BAD COP, BAD COP

Other books in the Virgin True Crime series

BAD COP, BAD COP

A Badge, A Gun and No Mercy

Edited by
Jack Sargeant

First published in 2003 by

Virgin Books

Thames Wharf Studios
Rainville Rd
London W6 9HA

Broken Teeth, Broken Bones and Broken Laws © Jack Sargeant
Another Brick in the Law © Chris Barber
Investigating Officer X © Martin Jones
La Noir: Whose Law? © Chris Barber
Fear and Loathing in California © Chris Barber
The Blue Wall of Silence © Russell Gould
Denis Tanner and The Bonnie Doon Bodies © John Harrison
Death Under the Influence © Mikita Brottman
Murderous Obsession © Mikita Brottman
Murder Frenzy © Mikita Brottman
Black Mother © Simon Whitechapel
The Way of the Flesh © Jack Sargeant
Force Versus Theory © Lance Sinclair

The right of the above authors to be identified as the Authors of the
Work have been asserted by them in accordance with the Copyright,
Designs and Patents Act 1988.

ISBN 0 7535 0776 5

Typesetting by TW Typesetting, Plymouth, Devon

Printed and bound by Mackays of Chatham PLC

CONTENTS

BROKEN TEETH, BROKEN BONES AND BROKEN LAWS

AN INTRODUCTION TO BAD COPS
Jack Sargeant

The only good cop is a dead cop.

Anon

However low a man sinks he never reaches the level of the police.

Quentin Crisp

Cops are boundary figures. Like the criminals they are meant to hunt, they inhabit a grey, twilight world: a zone in which those elements normally excluded or repressed by society – brutality, violence, human frailty and degeneracy – are exposed in harsh chiaroscuro. This is a world in which humanity comprises villains and victims. Is it any wonder the line can become blurred?

The fantasy of the police is always one of power, from *The Sweeney*[1] to *Dirty Harry*[2] to the leather fetish cops of Tom of Finland's hyper-masculine gay porn.[3] Real cops are self-appointed protectors, self-appointed upholders of 'the law' (a term so vague as to be redundant);[4] that many who choose this path are beholden to a belief in the power of justice is inevitable.[5] Yet such power is never assured, it is too fleeting, too vague, too transitory. Cops may want power but in actuality they have little.[6] Some cops feel forced to enact their own versions of justice, whether from frustration at watching the criminals walk free, or from an atavistic desire to make anyone suffer, even if only for a few hours, simply because they *want and demand* respect. They may have once wanted justice, but too often they will settle for violence and vengeance.

This volume focuses on bad cops; those rogue police officers that exist in their own, twisted world. The bad cops in this volume come from a variety of cultures. Far more could have been included but for spatial considerations. Bad cops are police officers who have gone too far even in the brutal world of law enforcement. Bad cops are police officers who have taken the law into their own hands. Bad cops are police officers who have framed innocent members of the public. Bad cops are police officers who have raped and tortured and killed, either because they are enamoured by the power of their position, or because they were already crazed and have used their position as a way to indulge their psychopathic tendencies.

Bad cops are cops who do bad things *because they can*.

Finally, however, is it possible to live in a cop-free world? People cannot be trusted. Anybody who doubts that should witness the mobs such as those who gather outside the trials of particularly brutal criminals, or those who threaten, and even attack, members of the community they suspect of crimes.[7] Modern history is punctuated with such events, from the lynch mobs of nineteenth- and twentieth-century USA, who dragged black suspects from their homes then tortured and hanged them, to the killings in townships in South Africa, where flaming tyres are placed over the screaming victim's head, burning the victim alive as he chokes on the heavy rubber smoke. Lynch mob justice has no court of appeal. Thus it is a necessity of our culture that the police exist.

The essays in this volume can be broadly divided into two perspectives. First, those which explore the police as innately corrupt – a dark, vile corruption that exists and spreads through certain squads, specific shifts, entire forces and even whole cultures. These essays see the police as filling a murky role that is framed within an oppressive socio-political context, keeping communities and criticism brutally suppressed.

Second, those which focus on individual cops who break rules, who pursue their own agenda with a dogged brutality. Some of these cases 'merely' reveal the general corruption and prejudices commonly associated with police culture, while others focus on police officers who would appear to be dangerously psychopathic. These are the brutal cops who respect nobody and seek nothing but their own satisfaction. What becomes terrifying while reading this volume is how often these feral, lone-wolf cops can count on the support of colleagues and law enforcement officials – in numerous cases explored here, those accused of brutality and depravity find support among those who should seek out corruption.

ACKNOWLEDGEMENTS

Thanks to all the contributors to this volume who have risen so willingly to the tasks laid before them, and who have unflinchingly – enthusiastically even – delved into tales of brutality and conspiracy. Special thanks to Kerri Sharp at Virgin who has, once again, encouraged a book that arrived late and is full of brutal stories. Additional thanks as ever to Monte Cazazza who shared many valuable insights into the human condition while I was editing this book, to Andrew Leavold for his endless enthusiasm, and to everybody in Sydney who looked after me while I edited and compiled the bulk of this volume. Special thanks also to those friends who have tolerated manias and rages, smiling through more bullshit than they deserved, and to Roslyn Lister who gleefully helped find research materials and who took me to the Justice and Police Museum.

A note on the text: The views expressed in these essays do not necessarily reflect those of other contributors, the editor, or the staff at Virgin Books. Readers are assumed to be able to make up their own minds and think for themselves.

NOTES

1. *The Sweeney* (1975) was a cult TV show. Notorious for its gritty authenticity, it counted many police officers among its fans.

2. *Dirty Harry* (Don Siegel, 1971) was the first – and best – of the series of Harry Callahan movies starring Clint Eastwood. Harry breaks a few laws, and a few heads, on the way, but he gets the job done.

3. Tom of Finland produced many illustrations of muscular men for various gay erotic titles – a fan of butch clones, an archetype image in his work is the brutal cop.

4. 'Law', 'justice', the 'common good', *et al.* are ultimately vague metaphysical terms. While culturally people are encouraged to view them as fixed absolutes, these are abstract concepts that merely reflect the interests of specific sectors of society (government, media, the masses, the individual) and are actually fluid, and open to multiple interpretation and schizophrenic etymology.

5. Those who apply for jobs in the police clearly believe in the importance of the role; however, it is not – and never will be – an easy job.

    It is notable that when faced with protesters chanting 'PIG' at demonstrations in the late 1960s several police officers and departments commented that 'PIG' stood for 'Pride, Integrity, Guts'. The police response to the insult is explored in, for example, 'The Power of Identity' in *Police Magazine*, August

2000, online at www.polfed.org/magazine and 'PIG PEN, PIGS and proud' in *OffBeat* at www.info.gov.hk/police/offbeat/archives/676/022e.htm, while there is also a law enforcement webring based on the slogan 'Pride, Integrity, Guts'.

6. The classic quote: 'The justice system is letting us down. We do all the leg work, arrest the criminals, and charge them. But the courts pass a mediocre sentence, and they're soon back at it . . . We put our lives at risk, for what? Me and my partner spotted a car with local criminals and tried to stop it, but as I approached they ran over me. We managed to find them – the main guy has been arrested and released six times. It's demoralising' (anonymous police officer quoted in Roger Graef, 'Whose Side Are You On?' *The Guardian*, 24 November 2001, www.guardian.co.uk).

7. Most notoriously in Britain this happened on the Paulsgrove housing estate in Portsmouth during the summer of 2000. Here, a gang of predominantly shrieking women and children formed an anti-paedophile mob and subsequently drove five inno-cent families from their homes, merely because the mob *suspected* these families of harbouring sex offenders. These suspicions were described by the police as being nothing other than 'gossip and rumour', and the police emphasised this during the protests.

   Such was the hysteria sparked by rumours and the tabloid press, who were engaged in a misguided sex-offender 'name-and-shame' campaign, that vari-ous innocent people were badly beaten by mobs in other areas of Britain, including a 67-year-old man. To confirm the terrifying stupidity of mob rule a paediatrician was driven from her home by an attack from people who evidently confused the words paediatrician and paedophile (Rebecca Allison, 'Doctor Driven Out of Home By Vigilantes', *The Guardian*, 30 August 2000, www.guardian.co.uk).

1. ANOTHER BRICK IN THE LAW

MET. DETECTIVE SERGEANT CHALLENOR, BUILDING UP EVIDENCE
Chris Barber

CHALLENOR: You're fucking nicked, me old beauty . . . Don't say please to me, my old darling.

11 July 1963[1]

TRUSCOTT: You're fucking nicked, me old beauty. You've found to your cost that the standards of the British police force are as high as ever.

Loot by Joe Orton, 1966[2]

Detective Sergeant (Second Class) Harold 'Tanky' Challenor, of West End Central (Savile Row) constabulary, was something of a local hero around his home-turf – London's Soho, in the early 1960s. The press frequently applauded his vigilant crusade against crime in lurid headlines. His superiors and colleagues in the Met admired his record-breaking number of arrests and convictions. The judiciary praised his courtroom banter, homespun rapport, and ability to cajole juries. None forgot his distinguished war record, tactically gained behind enemy lines with the SAS. No one questioned the methods he employed to achieve his extraordinary success. When circumstances finally conspired, forcing the Government to examine Challenor's unique policing methods, a dozen innocent people were pardoned and released from prison. Parliament demanded public inquiries, policemen were jailed, and the Establishment closed ranks; while Challenor ended up in the madhouse – at Her Majesty's pleasure.

The Challenor case represents either a landmark or watershed in the annals of British justice. Yet the scandal that brought about Challenor's demise was only the tip of the iceberg. Challenor's wartime exploits earned him the nickname Tanky (of tank corps). Unfortunately for Tanky, his real name inspired the pejorative colloquialism 'doing a Challenor' – Metropolitan Police slang for taking bribes or acting mad to avoid prison. Whether Tanky 'did a Challenor' among his many misdemeanours remains contentious. Allegations were made but dismissed by official inquiry – or cover-up. Basically, Challenor earned his reputation as a super crime-stopper by planting weapons on suspects to secure convictions where real evidence was lacking; he also routinely beat up and intimidated suspects. But he finally blundered when he planted a weapon on Donald Rooum, a member of the National Council for Civil Liberties (NCCL, now Liberty). Playwright Joe Orton based his 'nasty cop' character, Truscott, on Challenor in his West End stage-hit *Loot*. Another Tanky eccentricity was his persecution complex, inspiring him to compare himself to Oscar Wilde!

CASE ONE: GANG WARFARE (Pedrini, Oliva, Ford, Fraser, Cheeseman)

On the evening of 21 September 1962, 22-year-old Riccardo Pedrini left his parents' house in Bloomsbury to meet his mates for a drink in the West End. Riccardo had grown up locally and worked in the family-owned restaurant.

He met Alan Cheeseman (a fellow homeboy, aged 20) in the Lorraine Club/Bar, and danced with another friend, Josephine Jennings. Other pals arrived later. At 11 p.m, Riccardo and Alan left the club with four acquaintances. They strolled along Old Compton Street, seeking fast food and cabs home. As they passed the Phoenix Club (strip joint), Riccardo and Alan lagged behind.

Suddenly two cops burst out from the shadows, grabbing Pedrini and Cheeseman. The other lads were nowhere to be seen as the bewildered friends were piled into a police van that sped off to West End Central police station. Duty PCs Legge and Wells were accompanied by Phoenix Club proprietor Wilfred Gardiner, who had pointed them out to police.

Upon arriving at the station they were dragged into the charge room and ordered to empty their pockets on to the desk. 'Why did you bring us here?' Cheeseman asked.

'You'll find out soon enough,' replied Legge, grinning. A well-built, clean-cut, plain-clothed man with dark hair appeared from the corridor, arrogantly smirking with overbearing authority. His name: Detective Sergeant Challenor.

'Do you know Oliva?' he demanded menacingly.

'No,' says Cheeseman.

Pow! Challenor whacks him in the face, ranting frantically about protection rackets. 'You know what I'm talking about. Don't go to sleep, my darling, I'm coming back!' He marches off, leaving Cheeseman speechless with shock.

Moments later, Challenor returns, now clutching handfuls of dangerous weapons. He drops an iron bar on Pedrini's property (on the desk), and a flick-knife on to Cheeseman's bits 'n' bobs. 'Sign for it, it's yours . . . better for you if you make a statement.' An adjoining cell door is flung open and Pedrini staggers out, his nose bleeding profusely.

Both prisoners are charged with possessing offensive weapons (despite their strenuous denials). They are held overnight and, next morning, they're joined in the cells by Johnnie Ford – one of their acquaintances the night before – who was arrested on Shaftesbury Avenue.

Another inspector was on duty when he was brought in, so Ford was only charged with demanding money with menaces. Not until three o'clock the following afternoon does any cop bother to inform their parents of the arrests.

A couple of days later, Joseph Oliva was nicked by Challenor and PCs Jay and Laing. As Oliva was dragged from his car, Challenor searched it. According to the arresting officers, Oliva was carrying a knife and a homemade petrol bomb, both of which were discovered in his car. Initially Oliva maintained both weapons were planted by cops but, fearing this wouldn't stand up in court, he later claimed the knife was dropped by a friend, but insisted that Challenor had brought the bomb.

Johnnie Ford lived next door to the Pedrinis and was casually acquainted with the whole family. Ford was engaged in a long-running feud with Gardiner (the Phoenix Club owner) that started when Ford applied for a bar job at the Phoenix and Gardiner refused to employ him. They were also in dispute over a girl working in the club. Whenever Ford and friends (Joseph Oliva and James Fraser) passed Gardiner's clubs, there was much macho posturing and taunting between Ford and Gardiner, which sometimes led to scuffles. In one incident, Gardiner's car was damaged, threats were exchanged, and both sides called the police. Another time, Ford wanted to press charges against Gardiner. The police escorted all parties to Savile Row but, en route, Gardiner (a police snitch, according to 'Mad' Frankie Fraser) harangued Ford, causing him to withdraw the charges.

Gardiner claimed the final 'gang member' was James Fraser. He was arrested, searched and charged, apparently in possession of a razor; again, he began insisting it was a police set-up, but bottled out in court.

On 6 December 1962, 'the gang of five' appeared in court together, charged with conspiring to obtain money with menaces. Further, Fraser, Pedrini and Cheeseman were charged with actually demanding money. Four of the five men were also charged with possessing offensive weapons. The trial lasted two weeks at the Old Bailey.

Challenor was in his element for his court appearance, conjuring up his Soho beat as a twilight world of warring mafias, sexual degenerates and drug-crazed, spiv street gangs. Judge, jury and the media must have known better but chose to applaud Challenor's immaculate performance, accepting his vivid accounts as gospel. The prosecution case rested solely on evidence from Challenor, Gardiner (who presiding Judge Maude referred to as 'a ponce') and Gardiner's mistress, Elizabeth Evans. Gardiner claimed the Ford gang regularly threatened him in the street, and that Pedrini sliced his ear with a knife on the night of their arrest. In his defence, Pedrini's dance partner (on that night) testified he wasn't carrying a weapon when they smooched.

The verdict is guilty. Fraser is sentenced to fifteen months (for the lesser offence), while of the other four, for possessing weapons and demanding money with menaces, Pedrini gets seven years; Cheesmen, three years; Oliva and Ford each take five years' incarceration.

WHO DARES WINS

Harry Gordon Challenor was born on 16 March 1922 in a slum district of Bradley, Staffordshire. His father was, 'not to put too finer point on it, a bastard – a mean, cruel sadistic tyrant who terrorised his family,'[3] prepared to take a swing at his wife or son, whenever the mood took him. In his memoirs, Harold admits to nurturing a deep-seated hatred of his old man. His schooling was elementary and Harold took jobs as a male nurse, lorry driver and motor mechanic before turning twenty, when he enlisted in the army. He soon distinguished himself as a model soldier, winning selection to the SAS (Special Air Services).

During the war, Challenor was part of an elite commando force parachuting behind German and Italian lines on clandestine sabotage missions. He was renowned for his tactical ability and camaraderie when in the firing line. But, eventually, a mission into Italy went wrong, leaving Challenor a lone survivor. He was captured and tortured, but engineered his escape. Linking up with the Italian partisan resistance, Challenor was in his element, vigilantly charging around incognito, blowing up troop trains and wrecking enemy communications. Upon returning, he achieved the rank of company quartermaster sergeant and was awarded the Military Medal.

After leaving the army he joined the Flying Squad and, following several years' service, was promoted to Detective Sergeant Second Class and appointed to West End Central police station in 1962. One of his duties was to select, subordinate and train young PCs as potential tyro detectives.

CASE TWO: 'ELLO, 'ELLO, 'ELLO . . . (Wallace Gold)
Wallace Gold had a small dairy outlet in Soho and rented out an unused room over his shop. On 1 November 1962, Challenor appeared on his doorstep, asking after a tenant. Gold invited him in but Challenor eyed Gold suspiciously, referring to him as 'my old fruit'. It transpired that Gold's tenant had been involved in a recent heist of cigarette lighters. Challenor was shown the rented room, invited to search it, and allowed to wander freely around Gold's own rooms. Tanky instigated two prolonged searches of the building,

without Gold objecting. Bingo! In the tenant's chamber, Tanky finds a crate of the stolen lighters. He then wanders up to Gold's rooms, and is noted twiddling with a pack of Gold's cigarettes on the sideboard. Then he wanders out without saying a word. Next thing, Challenor's back, straight over to Gold's sideboard and ' 'ello, 'ello, 'ello, what's all this then?' From Gold's fag packet, Tanky produces one of the lighters.

Gold is nicked and interrogated in custody for several hours before being allowed to phone a solicitor – by which time it is 8 p.m. and too late. When he finally sees a solicitor after a night in cells, Gold protests his innocence. The solicitor tells him the court will not believe him and he should plead guilty, for a lenient sentence. Eventually Gold agrees, appearing at London Sessions in January 1963, and receiving nine months for handling stolen goods. Incidentally, later that day, Challenor escorted the tenant into the same court, where he owned up to purloining the lighters, without implicating Gold. Double whammy – Tanky gets the real thief knocked up as well!

Rumour has it that Challenor suspected Gold knew more about the lighter theft than he was telling. So Tanky decided to teach him a lesson.

COP DRAG ACT

Challenor was a workaholic and determined to top his military achievements with vigilant and unorthodox policing methods:

On one occasion he persuaded a small-time crook to take him to a criminal's pub so that working villains could be pointed out to him. Since the man was not prepared to be seen with a policeman, Challenor got hold of a woman's wig, borrowed one of Dorris's [his

*wife's] longest skirts, a roll-neck sweater, high-heeled
shoes, nylon stockings and a cloak-like coat and
handbag. Heavily made-up, he sat nursing his gin and
tonic while the villain nodded at the professional
heisters and hoisters present. Challenor's cover was
nearly blown when he entered the gents by mistake and
told a startled drinker: 'I've recently had a miscarriage
and must still be a bit light-headed.' He was even
propositioned and rescued by his 'boyfriend' for the
night, who kept up the deception and called him a 'silly
old cow'.*

The Underworld by Duncan Campbell[4]

After such excursions, Tanky sounds like a jovial
eccentric. But from his earliest days at Savile Row, he
weren't acting right! He lived with his wife in the Kent
countryside – and every night after work in the West
End, he insisted on walking home. Further, he frequently complained of deafness in one ear (usually as an
excuse for his spoilt-child-like temper rages, which
frequently intimidated suspects).

CASE THREE: GAMBLING WITH THE LAW (Lionel King and David Silver)

Challenor had enjoyed the media limelight of being
portrayed in the press as London's top gangbuster, a
self-styled Eliot Ness, leading The Untouchables. But by
25 April 1963, the attention was fading, so Tanky
arrested Lionel King – an employee of a Soho gambling
chain – along with David Silver, a friend of King's, who
happened to be in his car when Challenor pounced.

Sometime prior to King's arrest, Challenor had approached him to become a police informer, hoping to
cash in on King's rapport with notorious Soho villains
who used his bookmaking service. King laughed at

Tanky, and declined. Challenor was furious at his rejection and flew into a rage, promising King trouble. When King parked up, Tanky was waiting with PCs Jay and Etheridge, who pulled the driver and passenger aside for questioning, while Challenor suspiciously fumbled with the car-seat cushions . . . Surprise! His efforts uncover explosive detonators, hidden under a cushion.

Both King and Silver were charged with possession of offensive weapons. The only prosecution witnesses at the trial were three corroborating police officers, but the case hit the headlines shortly after a series of gang-related explosions hit Soho's bookmakers, arousing the public's fascination in gangland wars. The defence claimed the detonators were planted, but the jury decided the suspects were guilty. King got a two-year prison sentence, and Silver six months.

CRAZY HARRY CONTRA MONDEM!

'Your Uncle Harry . . .' was Challenor's preferred intro-duction to prisoners. When it came to interrogating suspects, Challenor played good cop and bad cop, a one-man show, oscillating between intimidation and rapport, usually addressing his prisoners as 'my old beauty' or 'my darling'.

He developed his own concept of justice and methods of detection. This involved ignoring the traditional system of following up crime reports in favour of getting out and searching for culprits. Having selected and arrested his villain, he would return to HQ, where he'd amassed an impressive selection of weapons (in his draw or locker), one for every occasion. These were dropped in front of prisoners with his customary punchline, 'That's yours, sign for it.'

In his memoirs, *Tanky Challenor*, he recounts:

> *I arrested more criminals in my period of service than any other officer. None of it was accomplished by unlawful acts, but by the cultivation and use of informants. They trusted me and knew I would never let them down. The men of violence were my target.*

But he admits:

> *I think it was Wilde who said that all men kill the thing they love, and I certainly did that . . . I accept that my illness may have resulted in me approaching my work with a crusading zeal . . . If I feel an attack coming on I take my pills . . .*[5]

CASE FOUR (and more): THE RIGHT TO REMAIN SILENT (Ernest Pink, Robert Brown, Frederick Bridgeman, William Francis and friends)

These four were arrested at Soho's Establishment Club on 25 May 1963 and charged with the usual – possessing offensive weapons. Pink was deaf and dumb, and Brown was deaf. All four of them tried to join a Soho club and were admitted by the doorman. When it was realised they weren't members, someone panicked and called the cops to eject them. Tanky was there in a flash, accompanied by a dozen officers, catching the four lads on the stairs. Challenor would claim in court that he confronted Pink, ordering him to take his friends outside. Pink apparently ignored the instruction and made 'offensive signs with his hands'. So, under Challenor's orders, the boys in blue returned 'offensive signs' with their boots. Dragged into the street, the four were searched and, low and behold, Pink was carrying a razor, Brown had a flick-knife, Bridgeman possessed a stiletto, and Francis was concealing a hatchet. All denied possessing weapons and all the prosecution witnesses were cops – six of them. Quite why none of the gang had used the weapons during the struggle was not considered at the Old Bailey. Pink (the only one with a previous criminal record) got three years, the other three each got one year.

During their preliminary hearing at Marlborough Magistrate's Court, four of Pink's pals turned up to offer moral support. Braggins, Matthews, Ireland and Steel were also deaf. During proceedings, Challenor noticed them in court and claimed they were making 'threatening signs'. So they were nicked and charged with conspiring to pervert the course of justice. All were refused bail. Steel got sixteen days, Braggins and Matthews got seventeen days a piece, while Ireland landed three weeks inside.

BLOWING THE WHISTLE ON TANKY

Gangland Soho may well have offered Challenor an ideal location to appeal to the public imagination with his creative embellishments. The metropolitan public – even judges and magistrates – who piled into Soho to chill out on Jazz, eat in the world's finest restaurants, or be seduced by spectacular stage shows, were either lacking brain cells or knew, deep-down, that the sleazy porn merchants and gangland gamblers only represented a tiny contingent in the bohemian heartland. But that actuality was too obtuse; people wanted Soho to evoke danger and excitement, a subterranean criminal empire. So they chose to patronise Challenor's sense of drama. Thus it was Challenor and his crime-busting cohorts in the Met who were believed in court; not the numerous young, sometimes foreign and usually working-class lads, who insisted they were set up. But Challenor was about to utilise his tried and tested methods in an alternative setting – a political demonstration – and his first victim was going to blow the whistle on his unorthodox approach to policing.

CASE FIVE: BRIC-A-BRAC (Donald Rooum, John Apostolou, Ranald Ede, Gregory Hill)

In July 1963, Her Royal Majesty Queen Frederika of Greece hit London on a high-profile state visit. Greece was seen as a very dodgy place at that time: authoritarian, autocratic, corrupt, oppressive . . . In particular, its police force largely comprised corrupt, neo-fascist thugs, employing violence to control and coerce the poverty-stricken majority of citizens. Human rights were dirty words; trade unionists, democrats and social reformists frequently 'disappeared' or had accidents in police custody. Many Greeks had split, preferring to live in exile in other European democracies – including London (renowned for its justice, fairness and honourable police force!).

So when a Greek head of state was welcomed in the UK, she was pursued by hordes of demonstrators protesting against everything she represented. Her presence at Claridges Hotel on 11 July attracted a large crowd of protestors, essentially peaceful, but shouting insults, waving banners and creating a harmless nuisance in the surrounding streets. One of these people was Donald Rooum, a professional cartoonist and NCCL/Liberty activist.

The police were out in force, intent on preventing protestors from expressing themselves in the royal presence. Extra officers had been drafted in for duty with nice overtime bonuses. Among them was Detective Sergeant Challenor, posted with three other detectives to keep an eye out for rambunctious protestors. Being an arch-royalist, Challenor regarded protest against a queen as a personal affront. He hadn't a clue about Greek politics and clandestine police agendas; he didn't need to, he had his own programme and tactics.

Rooum certainly wasn't an obstreperous demonstrator; he held back by the police line, quietly clutching his home-made paper banner, which read 'LAMBRAKIS RIP'. Suddenly, four plain-clothes cops were upon him, snatching his banner. 'Can I have my banner back?' he asked politely.

'You're fucking nicked, my old beauty,' replied the officer in charge, as Rooum was grabbed by the collar and jostled into a parked van. Back at West End Central, Rooum was escorted upstairs with clouts to his ear and was knocked to the floor, then frogmarched into the detention room, where Challenor continued to assault and insult him. Next, Challenor produced a package from his own pocket, wrapped in crumpled newspaper. Unwrapped, it revealed a piece of brick.

Meanwhile, Challenor was having a field day, returning sharpish to the demo and nicking a few more 'beauties' before the day was out – including two minors (under sixteen) whom he kindly provided with a bit of brick each. John Apostolou was arrested first, then two juveniles together, Ranald Ede and Gregory Hill.

All four were charged with possessing offensive weapons (bits of brick, supposedly to chuck at the royal). Each strenuously denied the charge from the start, claiming they were fitted up at the police station. The PCs assisting Challenor making the arrests were Baites, Oakey and Goldsmith. The same officers also arrested another four suspects – another (unnamed) juvenile, Colin Derwin, and John and Ronald Ryall. (Likewise they were charged with possessing bits of brick, which they maintained were planted by the cops.)

Poor Ede and Hill, it really wasn't their day. They had nothing to do with the demonstration when they were arrested. They were playing tennis that afternoon, and their family homes happened to be near Claridges. They were surprised to find police roadblocks halting their usual short cut home but, rather than taking a longer route, they decided to try to pass the police cordon with a group of protestors; not that such incidental details ever bothered Challenor in the course of his duties. Because they were under sixteen, they faced proceedings in a juvenile court (and the press was prohibited from revealing their names, adding to confusion) when Challenor's exploits hit the media, prior to completion of their hearing. Just as well, because after preparing a vindictive case against them, the prosecution advocated its intention not to pursue it.

Despite Challenor's excessive physical and psychological violence while interrogating Rooum, the cartoonist refused to sign a statement claiming the brick was his. For once, Challenor's punishment (or accidental oversight) meted out to the suspect turned out to be a blessing in disguise. Challenor neglected to bail Rooum, leaving him to spend the night in a cell. When Rooum was finally allowed a phone call, he rang his wife, who promptly contacted the NCCL, ensuring a top-notch solicitor appeared at the cells next morning to represent him. Mr Stanley Clinton Davis sorted bail at £10, escorting his client from police custody and immediately insisting on a change of clothes, taking possession of Rooum's suit, worn since the demo. Davis then phoned the Metropolitan Police forensic laboratory, asking them to test the suit for brick dust. (It's rare, but not unheard of, for police forensic scientists to prepare evidence for defence cases.) But Davis had second thoughts, realising that Challenor would have to take the suit to the lab himself. Instead, Davis carried the clothes to an independent laboratory.

This attention to detail established an airtight alibi and cast-iron defence case. When Rooum's barrister, Mr Michael Sherrard, was briefed, he had the crucial results of a rigorous scientific analysis of Rooum's clothes on the day of his arrest. The report concluded Rooum could not possibly have been carrying the said brick bit in that suit pocket without it crumbling and leaving dust traces. But there were no such traces. What's more, the scientist – Mr KF Kayser – realised that the type of brick concerned (from Marston Valley Brickworks, trade dealers) would necessarily strain the suit-pocket lining, causing scratches in the material. There were absolutely no such signs in the pocket, nor brick grains or fibres. Further (as Kayser would later testify at the trial), dust particles he retrieved showed it was not possible that any dust had recently been removed or any attempt made to clean the garment.

Rooum had an advantage over Challenor's preceding victims: he was a middle-class professional and well connected with the NCCL. The circumstances of Rooum's case were coincidentally fortuitous for the NCCL, because Challenor's activities had already reached their attention. Friends and relatives of prisoners, who maintained their innocence against Challenor's evidence, had contacted the organisation for help. Despite NCCL's attempts to have these cases reviewed, the Home Office consistently declined to take action, claiming insufficient evidence. Here was the opportunity Liberty had waited for.

Rooum's hearing was set for 19 July. However, Challenor was conspicuously absent from court, forcing the prosecution to ask for a recess (Challenor being the main prosecution witness). The magistrate complied, scheduling the case to be resumed on 8 August. While leaving the court, Rooum's disappointed council bumped into Challenor, heading for another case. They pleaded with him to visit the magistrate and ask him to resume the case immediately. Challenor became agitated, refusing outright to co-operate.

Three weeks later, Rooum's case resumed at Marlborough Magistrate's Court, with Kayser giving defence evidence as an independent forensic scientist. As a further precaution, the defence put Challenor through a gruelling cross-examination. But the finest defence stunt was held back for their summing up. In a spectacular display of courtroom drama, which outmatched any of Challenor's dramatic tirades, the defence produced before the court two further lumps of brick: one being the prosecution evidence from Ede's case; the second was apparently found in Hill's possession. These were placed alongside the brick supposedly from Rooum's pocket. Hoop-la! The three separate lumps matched together exactly, producing the complete brick.

The magistrate, Mr Robey, surveyed his courtroom while fumbling with the brick bits, noting the incontrovertible fact of their crumbling in his hands at the slightest touch. 'Not guilty, case dismissed!'

Mr Robey went on to refuse Rooum costs for expenses. What's more, he later presided over John Apostolou's case, facing the same charge and based on evidence of the same Detective Sergeant, in the same court, with almost the same brick bit as the prosecution's evidence. And Robey found Apostolou guilty as charged, fining him £10.

DOING A CHALLENOR

After August 1963, the repercussions of Rooum's brick case (and seven other Challenor 'brick bit' arrests from the protest) were finally attracting attention and embarrassing the Home Office. The NCCL pursued other unsound convictions pertaining to Tanky, and Rooum claimed damages. The media were asking questions. Police from outside Challenor's jurisdiction were ordered in to investigate. Tanky was given sick leave from September and, weeks later, suspended from duty. Yet he continued to drop into the police station and frequent his usual Soho haunts – doubtless returning to the scenes of his crimes! In December, believing himself to be invincible, he apparently leapt out in front of a moving vehicle (with no serious injury).

Eventually, crown prosecutor Mr John Mathew prepared a case against Challenor and his cohorts, PCs David Oakey, Frank Battes and Keith Goldsmith (who were under Challenor's charge). The charge was all too familiar to Tanky: conspiring to pervert the course of justice, specifically regarding the eight brick-bit busts. Proceedings started in March 1964 at Marlborough Street Magistrate's Court. Tanky had regularly appeared there in the witness box. Now he was in the dock, facing his former magistrate/fan, Mr Robey.

Rooum was called as a prosecution witness – despite his protestations that, on principle, he did not want to help send anyone to jail (regardless of what Challenor had done to him). Now the pressure was mounting on Challenor, who collapsed during proceedings and was escorted from the courtroom by a doctor. When the case resumed, all four cops were sent to the Old Bailey.

Come May, Challenor was still considered unfit to appear, so Mr Justice Lawton granted the prosecution request for a medical examination. When sessions resumed on 4 June, Dr William Calder testified that Challenor was mentally unfit to stand trial, backed by an independent doctor. Doctors claimed Challenor was a paranoid schizophrenic, and had been mentally unstable and potentially dangerous for some time.

Tanky was sent to a mental hospital for treatment, held at Her Majesty's pleasure.

Police officers coined the expression 'doing a Challenor', henceforth used to refer to bent coppers. PCs Oakey and Goldsmith were each banged up for four years (reduced to three on appeal) and Battes got three years.

It was alleged that Challenor took bribes. Although not substantiated by investigation, it was not rigorously refuted. Cheeseman's father claims he paid Tanky £50 for not opposing his son's bail. Apparently Challenor later phoned papa Cheeseman, demanding another £50; this was refused. Also, Fraser alleges he paid Tanky £100 not to reveal evidence concerning his apparent involvement in the conspiracy (with Pedrini etc.).

CASE SIX: BLACK MALE (Harold Padmore)

Padmore was an immigrant to the UK, born in Barbados; he had lived here many years, trouble free. He was once a renowned cricketer, but by July 1963, he was a London Transport shunter. His neighbour, Patricia Hawkins, worked in Soho 'sex bars' and had a reputation for fleecing customers.

When a Swiss tourist complained he was robbed by a couple of prostitutes, who took his cash and refused to have sex, the police arrested Hawkins (and her friend Jeanne Brown), installing them in cells at West End Central. Upon hearing this news, Padmore strolled over to the station and offered to post bail. Unfortunately, Tanky happened to be on duty.

Before he knew what hit him (literally), Padmore was beaten by Challenor and dragged up to the charge room by bobbies, bleeding from a broken tooth, while Tanky bawled 'coon,' and similarly tiresome clichés, between swigging gulps from a bottle of whisky. Other duty officers stood by, smirking. Challenor was probably inebriated and chanted racist rhymes like a soccer lout. When he tired of chanting and acting tough, he had Padmore banged up in a cell for the night, returning at 7 a.m. to turf the prisoner out after confiscating his diary and ordering him to return to the station at 7 p.m. for further questioning.

Twelve hours later Padmore dutifully showed up, accompanied by his solicitor. Tanky met him with two other officers, accusing Padmore of 'obviously taking part in a conspiracy'. Harold P. was informed he would be detained, until Challenor could be bothered to charge him. Padmore motioned to his solicitor to take his wallet, causing Tanky to lurch at him and forcibly curtail the transaction. Held overnight in a cell, Padmore heard an inspector enter the charge room, suggesting to Challenor that he might charge the prisoner, but was bluntly told he was 'too busy'. Next morning, Challenor rudely awakened Padmore with a left hook (a charge Challenor later denied); but it so happened on that morning that another prisoner remembered glancing a black man who worked for London Transport in an adjacent cell, with blood pouring from his nose. The observant prisoner was Donald Rooum.

On 8 January 1964, Padmore appeared at the Old Bailey with Hawkins and Brown. The prosecution alleged Padmore had conspired with the women, in a Soho 'clip joint' rip-off scam, brought to police attention by a Swiss victim. Padmore insisted he had nothing whatever to do with the club; he was just a friendly neighbour trying to do a good turn. This time, the jury could not agree a verdict, so a fresh trial was ordered. By the time this was scheduled, it was Challenor that the media and public wanted to see in the dock. The prosecution tactfully chose not to pursue the case and

Padmore was acquitted (and later awarded £500 damages).

PARDONS ALL ROUND

By late 1963, thirteen convicted prisoners claimed they had been framed by Challenor and his PCs. Cases were taken up by Liberty and lawyers, who lobbied Parliament and the Home Office, and appealed for appeals. Martin Ennals was a prominent NCCL activist, while prisoners' determined friends and families fought for justice. Then there were the eight brick-bit arrests, including juveniles, fairly claiming they were set up, having charges against them dropped during proceedings, or having already served jail sentences.

Rooum issued a writ against Challenor, claiming damages for assault and wrongful arrest, false imprisonment and malicious prosecution; he was awarded £500.

Henry Brooke, the Home Secretary, finally made a statement on the Challenor cases on 2 July 1964, claiming, 'by excessive devotion to duty and overwork in the police service', Challenor had suffered a mental breakdown. Further, he named twelve convictions secured by Challenor where gross injustices *may* have arisen: King, Silver, Ryall, Ryall, Derwin, Pedrini, Ford, Cheeseman, Oliva, Fraser, Louciades and Gold, announcing five free pardons, five referrals to the Court of Criminal Appeal, and two cases where no further action was intended. Confronted with a barrage of questions and insults from MPs, Brooke stated his intention to open two official inquiries into the affair.

CASE SEVEN: THE TAILOR'S NEW CLOTHES?
(Andreas Louciades)

Andreas Louciades was a local, prize-winning tailor with a distinguished clientele, but a few of his regulars were wealthy crooks and gangsters. In 1959 and earlier, he's known to have occasionally passed information to the police, helping their enquiries. But by 1963 he felt he had done his bit for 'justice' and wanted out with his cop associates. Tanky had planned to use him to obtain information on some dodgy deals going down and was infuriated by his refusal to help. 'You're in my territory now . . .' he warned Louciades. The tailor was unmoved by the cop's threats and, besides, Andreas wasn't planning to spend much time in Soho now; his sartorial reputation meant customers were prepared to travel to him.

By the evening of 17 August 1963, Louciades had avoided Soho, and Challenor, for some time. He met one of his customers in a Balham pub, the man owing his tailor cash for a suit. Another friend accompanied the customer, and the three of them sat in Louciades's car in the pub car park to discuss payments.

They were astonished when cops surrounded the car. Next thing, they were in custody, at West End Central. Louciades implored Challenor to explain why he was arrested. Tanky murmured he was in the company of a felon in the car. Clearly, thought Louciades, a misunderstanding had arisen, and he proceeded to explain the situation to his custodian with a relieved sigh. The disinterested cop suggests it's not that simple, because his car had been searched and a sack of housebreaking implements had been discovered in his boot. What's more, the chap owing him suit money was wanted 'very badly' for something, and that if Louciades were released, they would have to drop charges against the 'wanted' man as well. No, best if they all appeared in court together, charged with housebreaking.

And so it goes . . . Louciades appeared at London Sessions in September alongside the other two (despite their insistence Louciades was not involved with them) and was duly sentenced to two concurrent eighteen-month prison sentences.

THE BROADER IMPLICATIONS

One genuine crook acquainted with Tanky is ex-Richardson gang henchman Frankie Fraser, who says in *Mad Frank's Diary*:

> I'd known Challenor . . . he came sniffing round, but . . . we sent him on his business. Challenor had been going mad for months, if not years, and he thought he was a one-man campaign to clean up Soho. When he was in court he made it sound like Chicago in the days of Al Capone and what was worse everyone believed him . . . in them days who was going to believe a young kid against a war hero?
>
> Challenor got all the praise from the press . . . and what's worse he got a licence to go round fitting people up . . .
>
> And Challenor went on and on. He did all this in front of other officers, who didn't stop him.
>
> . . . he was found unfit to plead and had a short spell in hospital. After that I heard he'd got a job as a solicitor's clerk over South London.[6]

The Challenor Case exposed not only the police, but the whole British legal establishment (judges and magistrates, court process and juries, the Home Office and legal apparatus) to serious re-examination.

The number of pardons for wrongful imprisonment has soared in recent years. If there were any significant changes after Challenor, it was too little, too late. Tinkering with the system by successive regimes has not delivered. Only a complete and radical overhaul of the whole caboodle might restore faith in justice (like Bertrand Russell's suggestion, that Britain needs a second police force, whose sole function is to prove the innocence of suspects). This just isn't going to happen. But there's an alarming warning for us all in this highly flawed criminal justice system. Fitting up innocent people for unsolved crimes could happen to anyone, from school kids playing tennis, to deaf mutes watching a public trial . . . to *you*.[7]

BIBLIOGRAPHY

AJ Ayer, *Russell*, London: Fontana, 1972.

Duncan Campbell, *The Underworld*, London: Pengin Books and BBC Worldwide, 1994.

Harold Challenor (ex-Detective Sergeant) with Alfred Draper, *Tanky Challenor – SAS and The MET*, London: Leo Cooper, 1990.

Frankie Fraser with James Morton, *Mad Frank's Diary*, London: Virgin Books Ltd, 2000.

Mary Grigg, *The Challenor Case*, Harmondsworth: Penguin Books Ltd, 1965.

James Morton, *Bent Coppers*, London: Warner Books, 1993.

James Morton, *Gangland*, London: Warner Books, 1993.

Joe Orton, *Loot*, from *The Complete Plays*, London: Eyre Methuen Ltd, 1973.

NOTES
1. Mary Grigg, *The Challenor Case*, p. 50.
2. Joe Orton, *The Complete Plays*, p. 273.
3. Harold Challenor with Alfred Draper, *Tanky Challenor*, p. 21.
4. Duncan Campbell, *The Underworld*, p. 218.
5. Harold Challenor with Alfred Draper, *Tanky Challenor*, p. 199.

6. Frankie Fraser and James Mortom, *Mad Frank's Diary*, p. 189–91.
7. Quotes used throughout text, from custody/witness statements and trial transcripts, as recorded in Mary Grigg, *The Challenor Case*, except where otherwise stated.

2. INVESTIGATING OFFICER X

OPERATION COUNTRYMAN VS. THE METROPOLITAN POLICE
Martin Jones

Central London in the mid 1970s. Over the course of three years, three violent crimes take place in the city north of the River Thames:

- May 1976 – At the Fleet Street headquarters of the *Daily Express*, four gunmen steal £175,000 in employee wages.
- September 1977 – A security van delivering money to the Williams & Glyn City bank in Birchin Lane is ambushed by six masked gunmen. One guard is shot in the legs. The gang escape with £270,000.
- May 1978 – After a security van has been locked inside the loading bay of the *Daily Mirror* offices, three gunmen – two disguised as employees – attack it. The van's driver is shot at point-blank range and dies on the way to hospital. The robbers get away with an estimated £200,000 in wages.

No one was ever charged with the *Daily Express* robbery. After the Williams & Glyn job, eight known London criminals were arrested, but all of them – including Tony White, George Copley and Francis Fraser Junior (a relation of 'Mad' Frankie Fraser) – were freed on bail, and the following year every charge related to that case was dropped due to lack of evidence. Tony White was arrested again in June 1978, two weeks after the *Daily Mirror* robbery, along with one Billy Tobin. White made bail and subsequently had charges dropped against him. Tobin was later acquitted.

It seemed to all concerned that these three successful robberies were the work of a gang outside London. But, in the years immediately following the crimes, some would have you believe that the brains behind them were deep in the heart of the city, right at its lawful centre: anonymous, high-ranking police officers embroiled in criminal complicity and conspiratorial dealings. It was the 'Square Mile' robberies that were more or less directly responsible for the formation of the internal investigation known as Operation Countryman. An expensive and ultimately fruitless gesture, Operation Countryman was created ostensibly to dig out claims of corruption within the Metropolitan Police Department in the late 1970s. By its closure all the investigation had achieved was a few unrelated convictions, a deep mistrust between certain individual officers, and more fuel for the rumour mill it had uncovered.

ALL POINTS BLOCKED

Formed in 1829 through a Parliamentary Act enforced by the Home Secretary Sir Robert Peel, the Metropolitan Police force has not been without its share of internal dirt. Hardly surprising, considering it has 99 per cent of Greater London – and most of the suburbs – under its jurisdiction: an area of some 786 square miles (2,036 square kilometres). The Met's most infamous scandals appeared at either end of a hundred-year span: in 1877 conmen William Kurr and Harry Benson enlisted the services of bribable inspectors and lower ranks to act as 'early warning systems' for their crimes. In 1977 the Flying Squad subdivision – or 'Sweeney' (rhyming slang: Sweeney Todd – Flying Squad) – became the subject of investigations over officers taking cash gifts from Soho porn shop owners. Throughout the 1960s and 70s, the Metropolitan Police Department appeared to be staffed by hard-drinking, morally indifferent officers who thought nothing of taking cash from the highest, or lowest, bidder. After the Soho scandal, there was barely a chance for the Met to breathe before another incident surfaced to tarnish its already damaged reputation.

Following accusations made by criminal informers, in July 1978 the Commander of the Flying Squad, Don Neesham, filed a report to his superiors citing what he believed to be a 'corrupt association' between the armed men who had undertaken the Square Mile robberies and the City of London Police. A shortlist of officers' names was drawn up as evidence. Peter Marshall, Commissioner of the City force, asked New Scotland Yard to conduct an investigation into the claims; but, after obtaining further information, the Met's Complaints Investigation Bureau (CIB) decided that a force independent of London was needed to continue the process.

Marshall contacted the Home Office and, with the consent of the Home Secretary Merlyn Rees, invited Assistant Chief Constable Leonard Burt up from Dorset Constabulary to undertake the investigation. Burt brought with him a team of 30 officers and was appointed under Section 49 of the Police Act 1964. With headquarters set up in Camberwell Police Station (south of the Thames), his brief was given by the City force to investigate a number of specific complaints relating to alleged malpractice by City officers in connection with recent serious crimes. Operation Countryman was born.

A few weeks into the investigation, it became apparent that Metropolitan officers might possibly be involved alongside their City colleagues. The Deputy Commissioner of the Met, Patrick Kavanagh, asked Burt to extend his brief in order to look into the allegations. An unrelated scandal in 1970, after which the Met was rumoured to have closed ranks against outside investigators, was still fresh in Kavanagh's mind, and he was determined as much as the newly appointed commissioner Sir David McNee to erase this image, eager to have his force portrayed as open and willing to co-operate. But, despite the free hand offered by their hosts, it appeared that Burt and his superior, Chief Constable Arthur Hambleton, had different ideas as to where the Countryman investigation should take them. Hambleton, in particular, began to take an increasingly prominent role in the investigation.

From the start, they seemed to make things difficult for themselves: Met officers nicknamed the team 'The Sweedey', a tag that played on the provincial stereotype and doubts that they could cut it in the city (the official name of the investigation was chosen by Hambleton); and they gathered no allies by beginning a series of complaints about 'obstructions' made during the course of their work, the first of which being the allegation that there had been an attempt to interfere with records at their Camberwell HQ. Burt requested that his team be moved to a station outside the Metropolitan Police district. With the co-operation of Sir Peter Matthews, the Chief Constable of Surrey, Countryman was moved to Godalming Police Station, 30 miles (48 km) outside the capital. It was seen by senior officers as a terrific waste of time: staff now had to travel to and from London to Surrey, and a shorter working week was created due to having to go home on Friday afternoon and return on Monday morning.

But the Met stayed fast in their help; Kavanagh was still sensitive to his force's image, and let Countryman's autonomy ride for a while, neither asking for nor receiving any reports. Countryman's initial investigations were well publicised but hardly inspiring: they collected word-of-mouth accounts from criminals and 'supergrasses', but did not take any written statements at that point, an action that would come back to haunt them later. Because of the investigation's high profile, Countryman officers also began to receive many complaints against the Met and City forces that were unconnected with Leonard Burt's original brief. For reasons known only to himself, Burt did not pass on these complaints to the relevant forces for separate investigation, but decided to keep them within the net of Countryman. It was obvious to some observers that Burt saw the operation as an anti-corruption squad that he would sweep through the London forces, cleaning up in style. But, for all intents and purposes, the original aim had disappeared in Burt's eyes and he was now overwhelmed with evidence from all quarters. Instead of returning to the City brief, he – with the support of Hambleton – increased his team to 80 officers. This meant that provincial forces all over the south of England were depleted in order for Burt to cast his net wider.

Every complaint the team received was investigated, which did nothing more than push the original target further away; and not everything received could be called solid evidence: every criminal with an axe to grind, a grudge to sate, an officer to get one over on seemed to turn up at the Countryman HQ. Because of so much information streaming in, Burt requested a computer to store it on, an expensive matter in the 1970s. With an eye on the mounting cost, the Met provided them with one. Although every decision was made through Home Office consultation, the Met was still granting requests, worried about potential claims of interference.

At some point during the early stages of the investigation, Hambleton steered Burt towards the Flying

Squad and its subdivision, the Robbery Squad. Further complaints arose when it was discovered that Country- man detectives were muscling in on supergrass in- formers, the Robbery Squad's main vein of information. Enraged by this interference, Don Neesham – who had set the whole investigation rolling in the first place – made a complaint in November 1978 about their dealings with informers. Neesham's main problem with Countryman was the fact that they had been known to offer 'soft' options to informers, thus undermining the Robbery Squad's authority, knocking down any trust individual detectives had spent years building up.

As complaints were received from a small number of Sweeney officers over Countryman detectives approach- ing their informers, both Peter Marshall and David McNee wondered why they were being kept in the dark. They were not the only ones. In July 1979, Sir Thomas Hetherington, the Director of Public Prosecutions (DPP), met with McNee and Kavanagh to express his concern over the length of time Countryman was taking: he had his doubts over the expertise of Burt's team, and of their ability to provide any solid results. This was something McNee agreed with but, like Kavanagh, he knew it was no basis for interference from the Met. Instead, he diplomatically offered to lighten the burden of the Countryman team by taking away cases not related to the original brief. Burt refused the offer, on the grounds that all complaints and information had been passed to the team under the strictest confidence. It seemed that in his quest to drive out corruption, Burt saw all around him as potentially corrupt.

Elsewhere, the DPP found other problems: one of his officials, Kenneth Dowling, denied a request by a Countryman sergeant to interview a suspect in prison. The sergeant went ahead anyway, and the suspect,

George Copley (one of the men arrested in connection with the Williams & Glyn robbery), surreptitiously taped the interview. The tape was later produced at trial, showing that the sergeant had offered him a reduced sentence in return for admitting to the robbery and providing evidence of corruption among certain Met officers.

By October 1979, Kavanagh still could not see what Countryman had achieved, or where the investigation was heading. He told Hambleton and Burt as much, but all Burt could offer was that the DPP had hindered him by not making a decision on a Countryman report submitted twenty-two weeks earlier (McNee later heard that this was because the report had been inadequate). Burt resented the suggestion that he was hoarding information and running with enquiries that were far removed from his original brief. Hambleton acted as mediator and it was agreed that Kavanagh would regularly be kept up to date. But by the next month, neither Kavanagh nor McNee had received any new information on Countryman's progress. This led McNee – who, as Commissioner, was supposed to remain impartial – to write a letter of complaint to Hambleton.

In reply, Hambleton and Burt met with McNee, Kavanagh and the DPP at New Scotland Yard. Hambleton brought with him progress reports, with, he said, the rest to follow within a few days and the promise of regular reports from thereon. He also agreed that Countryman would not take on any new lines of enquiry without prior consultation. As a gesture of goodwill the DPP offered to provide a member of his staff to Countryman full time.

Within less than two weeks of the meeting, a report appeared in the *Sunday Times* stating that Burt was unhappy with the 'obstacles' being placed in the way of

Countryman by the Met and DPP. Angered by this rejection of his goodwill, on 7 December 1979 Kavanagh, along with the DPP and Ernest Bright (Assistant Commissioner of the City force), held a meeting with Hambleton. He was told that if he or Burt continued to make complaints about obstruction he would have to resign as head of the investigation. Unwilling to do this, Hambleton offered his co-operation in a venture that would put the investigation back on track. Together the four of them drew up a press statement to be released on the same day by Dorset Police, under Burt's name.

Among the seven points laid out, Burt was required to admit that some of the complaints investigated had been proved unfounded, that during the inquiry regular consultations were made with the DPP, and that accusations of obstruction were completely without grounds, with Countryman receiving full co-operation from the DPP and both Commissioners. 'My detectives are working extremely hard,' he stated:

> They are dedicated and have the will to succeed; they are undaunted by some reports that have appeared in the press and other media. Events in the future will prove that the Countryman team has been more than adequate for its task and that any difficulties they have encountered have been overcome.[1]

But this did not hide another point made on the statement: after over a year of investigations, only five Metropolitan officers had been suspended from duty, with only four subsequently made subject to further proceedings by the DPP. In the City force, only one officer had been charged. McNee called the claim made later by Hambleton on the *World In Action* television

programme (broadcast 20 July 1981) – that Countryman would have folded if he hadn't agreed to the
contents of the statement – 'nonsense'. Kavanagh told
McNee that at the time of the statement Hambleton had
alleged that Don Neesham had been 'unhelpful' towards
his team; but Hambleton produced no evidence to
support this. Nevertheless, still determined to have no
blemishes on his force, McNee saw that Neesham would
be moved to other duties. Instead, Neesham took early
retirement and resigned, leaving with more complaints
against Countryman. The Commissioner must have
wondered at what price his actions were placed,
especially when he and Kavanagh visited Countryman
HQ:

> I was not impressed. It seemed to me that the name of
> any police officer mentioned to members of the
> Countryman team, in conversations with criminals and
> others, was being fed into the computer. Wholly
> innocent officers were accordingly going into the pool of
> suspects, often only on the word of rogues. Far too
> much attention was being given to compiling a mass of
> intelligence, much of it of doubtful quality, and I was
> convinced that the team were being sidetracked from
> their primary objective. No arrests after many months
> of inquiry was not my idea of success.[2]

But a natural end came to Hambleton's reign when he
announced that he was to retire at the end of February
1980, although he did not leave without difficulties.
Hambleton took it upon himself to conduct an almost
exclusive vendetta against the DPP. The most serious
incident came when Countryman finally made its first
arrest of a Detective Inspector from the City force,
although the charge was unconnected to the original

brief. In blatant disregard for procedure, Leonard Burt bypassed the DPP and, with a Dorset solicitor, brought the case before a court in Hertfordshire. Magistrates there granted an application for the accused officer to be remanded in custody for three days and he was taken down to Dorset for the duration. On 18 February 1980, a representative of the DPP had to attend court to request that the prosecution be withdrawn due to inadequate evidence. With this one 'success' snatched away from him, Hambleton claimed that the whole of Countryman would be discredited, despite the fact that he had become a law unto himself when it came to running the investigation. He also claimed that the DPP was obstructing their progress, but again could offer no convincing examples. In a move strange for such outsiders in the capital, Burt ordered the DPP's representative at Countryman HQ to leave.

The representative stayed, but Hambleton left on 29 February, and Sir Peter Matthews took over responsibility for Countryman. Burt continued as its head until he too returned to Dorset in May 1980. With these two antagonists gone, Matthews quickly took charge: he cut the operation down to the terms of the original brief and passed all unconnected matters on to the Met CIB or the City force. He also brought in Deputy Assistant Commissioner Ron Stevenson, who had lengthy experience of corruption within the force, being a former head of the CIB. Eventually, eight Met officers were indicted, but none were convicted by the courts. Three were subsequently dismissed as a consequence of disciplinary proceedings taken by the Met, which had found them guilty of tampering with suspect interview records (one of the dismissed, Inspector James Jolly, had been separately tried and acquitted for attempting to frame one of the *Daily Mirror* robbery suspects, Billy Tobin), one resigned, and four resumed duties. But it was too little, too late. On 30 June 1982 Metropolitan Police involvement in Countryman officially ceased. The eventual cost of the operation came to £4 million.

Later, three senior officers on the original list of suspects were separately investigated by the CIB in regard to other offences, and this led to the conviction of two of the officers; but how these convictions came about adds another layer to the disordered workings of Operation Countryman.

OUTSIDERS ON THE SQUARE

On 1 June 1978, the day after the *Daily Mirror* robbery, Detective Chief Superintendent John Simmonds left the Met to become head of the Criminal Investigation Department at the City force. He was now in charge of 830 officers. Formed in 1839, the City force patrols the Square Mile of the capital on the north bank of the River Thames. Simmonds was a morally sound officer, and also a Freemason, but he walked into his job determined to keep quiet about his affiliation. He was well aware that the force was rife with the 'Brotherhood', and did not want to be accepted among his men purely on that basis. His superior, Peter Marshall, was a non-Mason, but both men had enough sense to realise that the City force, because of its independence and relatively small reach, was essentially inbred and closed to other forces. Simmonds suspected that this led to criminal co-operation among some of the officers, taking as an example the recent Square Mile robberies: three violent crimes executed successfully on City turf, and not one conviction between them.

For a while Simmonds maintained his bluff, until one day in September 1978 when City Detective Chief Inspector Phillip Cuthbert met a non-force friend of

Simmonds at a Masonic gathering, and inadvertently learned of his boss's ties with them. When Cuthbert confronted his superior, Simmonds admitted his membership but stated that he wanted to keep it to himself. This had no effect on the garrulous Cuthbert, and soon enough Simmonds detected a more relaxed atmosphere among his new colleagues. DCI Cuthbert was Master of Lodge No. 3475 (Waterloo), but there was a reason beyond Masonic business for his ingratiation into Simmonds's world: Cuthbert had discovered that *his* name was on the shortlist of officers put forward by Don Neesham in relation to the Square Mile robberies. It was time for the Brotherhood to do him some favours.

Bypassing police rank, Cuthbert approached Simmonds 'on the square'; that is, as a fellow Mason bound by the same rules of secrecy. Cuthbert wanted to unburden himself of something, and Simmonds agreed to meet up in a pub a few days later. But the lawman in Simmonds suspected a deeper agenda behind this, and so he told Commissioner Marshall about the meeting, who in turn contacted Operation Countryman. Together they agreed that Simmonds should go to the meeting wearing a concealed tape recorder and microphone. The 'wire' recorded a three-hour conversation involving Simmonds, Cuthbert, and two of his associates: Irving Shire (a solicitor's clerk) and Paul Davis (a solicitor). The finished tape would not be used until 1982, when Cuthbert and another officer appeared at the Old Bailey on bribery charges, the result of the CIB's investigations post-Countryman.

The Masonic links holding Operation Countryman up are hard to ignore. This is not to claim that Masons were under every stone on the investigation's path, but connections have been made between the two by numerous writers. Arthur Hambleton was also a Freemason but, like Simmonds, he fully understood the influence Freemasonry had on the police and refused to let it interfere with his Countryman quest (he did not join a lodge in Dorset until after he had retired from that force). According to Martin Short in *Inside The Brotherhood* (the follow-up to the late Stephen Knight's *The Brotherhood*):

> *It was later alleged that Freemasonry was not only involved in the corruption that Operation Countryman was investigating, but had later caused its overall failure by sabotage.*[3]

But Short goes on to state – rightly – that just because many crooked (and lawful) officers were Masons, it did not mean that the Brotherhood was behind it all. But, then again, absence of evidence does not mean evidence of absence. Stephen Knight's earlier book traces the root of Operation Countryman back to one man: the Commissioner of the City of London Police between 1971 and 1977, James Page.[4] It could be seen as a tenuous link, but Knight was a fervent man with a nose for conspiracies (his 1976 book *Jack The Ripper: The Final Solution* is one of the most convincing in that field), and Page's history adds more than a few pieces to the crimes that sparked Operation Countryman, the crimes that Hambleton quickly forgot in his own particular crusade.

After it was announced that the current Commissioner of the City Police, Arthur Young, was retiring, Chief Superintendent James Page was made Acting Commissioner in November 1969. Up to that point, Page had worked his way steadily through the ranks of the Met. Originally hailing from the Blackpool City force – which in the 1960s was under the command of the venal Chief Constable Stanley Parr – Page transferred to the Met as a Commander in 1967. Two years later he was promoted to Chief Superintendent. On the eve of his temporary Commissioner promotion, Page was visited by an anonymous, high-ranking officer. The officer warned him about two City officers – Knight calls them 'Oates' and 'Tearle' – whom he knew to be taking bribes off criminals in return for altering charges. With good humour, Page ignored these warnings; after all, it was addressed that the best way he worked with his men was on a grass-roots level: he liked to be known by everyone as 'Jim', and was an enthusiastic social drinker, with a reputation for turning up at even the smallest gatherings. Freemasonry must have seemed like a dozen hospitable doors opening to Page, and he was eventually admitted in the summer of 1971 to City Livery Club Lodge No. 3752. Around the same time he won the Commissioner's position, ahead of the other shortlisted – and favoured – candidate, the Deputy Assistant Commissioner (Metropolitan Training) John Alderson.

Page's promotion surprised many, especially when there had been better-suited candidates. Despite a number of professional achievements, and his popularity within the lower ranks of the force, Page was seen as unsuitable for the job: mainly because of his constant drinking, but also because the position was far above his abilities as an officer. Knight underlines the fact that Page's first allegiance was to the Masons, which perhaps goes some way to explaining how he got the job: the Brotherhood appealed to Page's nature on a surface level, i.e. if you were a police officer and a Mason then you were a good officer because Freemasonry was a benevolent organisation. Page drank with 'Oates' and 'Tearle', who were also – obviously – Masons. Within his own lodge, 'Tearle' was Worshipful Master, and so superior in rank to Page. Both 'Oates' and 'Tearle' were promoted a number of times under Page's guidance. This, it seemed, was the way the Masonic pyramid worked: influence and advantage trickling down from higher levels.

But some who caught the flow were not always made of the same material as men such as John Simmonds. According to Knight, 'Oates' and 'Tearle' had played a part in all three of the Square Mile robberies. They assisted with the *Daily Express* job, and helped set up the Williams & Glyn and *Daily Mirror* jobs. Masonic police shared out the proceeds between them, including around £60,000 from one job alone. Knight reasons these actions thus: if Page had *not* been a Mason, he would *not* have promoted 'Oates' and 'Tearle'. But they, and others, *were* (he concludes with the information that 'Tearle' remained in the force but 'Oates' left, possibly as the one officer who resigned after Countryman's closure). If the two officers were corrupt *and* trusted, that would lead to more complicity than among non-Masons. The problem, it seemed, stemmed not from these directly involved officers, but a superior such as James Page, whose lax attitude was the root of the problem, albeit unwittingly. Page, like Phillip Cuthbert, was a thorn in the side of Countryman, purely because of his Masonic connection. But Page was perhaps oblivious to what went on beneath him, whereas Cuthbert was using Freemasonry to dig himself out of a deep hole.

The significance of the connections between Masonry, Page and Cuthbert are that the Brotherhood's bonds of secrecy tend to rise above the common laws of England. Felony, however, is one of the acts these bonds do not apply to, so John Simmonds rose above *that* and decided that someone needed to be told. Meanwhile, Masons like Cuthbert and Page just sunk deeper into the arms of their corrupt brothers, with the latter forced to make an ignominious exit from the force in 1977, moving on to the Home Office (the late Page's family made complaints over his 'unfair and inaccurate' portrayal when *The Brotherhood* was published). As Short records in *Inside The Brotherhood*, Simmonds's decision to expose his criminal fellow Mason resulted in his ostracism from the Brotherhood: for other policemen, it was easier to turn a blind eye to what was happening within their own force.

A MEANS TO A LOOSE END

Where Countryman failed, the CIB succeeded. An unconnected conviction still had threads leading back to the original investigation brief but, by that time, it was too late to restart such a costly operation. DCI Phillip Cuthbert and Detective Sergeant John Goldburn were the two men successfully convicted. The trial began in June 1982 at the Old Bailey, and would hang Cuthbert up as an example, perhaps to cover the dead ends that had gone before him.

Simmonds's taped conversation with Cuthbert became the main evidence in the trial. He had dangled a microphone down into the Masonic depths of the Met and City forces and then plucked it out for the courts to listen to. At their pub meeting, Cuthbert took Simmonds into his confidence almost immediately, due to their Masonic connections. Cuthbert told him that an un-named senior officer (hereafter called 'Officer X'), at the time working on the Regional Crime Squad, was the mastermind of the *Daily Express* robbery, pocketing at least £20,000 from it. Cuthbert called him 'one of the greatest unhung villains'[5] in London, and alleged that this officer had also taken a bribe (or in police slang, 'a drink') from the Williams & Glyn robbery, despite having no direct involvement in it, legitimate or otherwise. The amount from that job to change hands within the force was, according to Cuthbert, between £60,000 and £90,000. When Simmonds questioned why the senior officer had received the bribe, Cuthbert explained:

> Because he was [Officer X] and because he worked with all of us, and, you know, he was in a position of power up there on the fucking Regional Crime Squad and covered things, same as all the blokes on the Robbery Squad had a drink out of it, going right up to the fucking top of the tree . . .[6]

Discussing the Williams & Glyn job, Cuthbert admitted he had some involvement in it, but nothing direct. All his actions were guided by Officer X: Cuthbert was just the man who handed over an envelope. And everyone profited, even a little. The curve of distorted evidence ran, it seemed, from the bottom to the top. And this was not Cuthbert's only crime: the tape revealed that he had given insurance reward money to various Scotland Yard commanders over the years.

As well as the tape, the court heard a statement from a junior officer who said that Cuthbert had paid him bribe money after the Williams & Glyn robbery, and also from criminal Alfie Sheppard, who had acted as middleman in negotiations between Cuthbert and the underworld concerning bail bribes and the watering-down of evidence connected with Williams & Glyn. Sheppard said that, on behalf of the Williams & Glyn suspects, he had handed over thousands of pounds to Cuthbert in a restaurant opposite Bishopsgate Police Station. But it was the tape that sent Cuthbert down, not just for his criminal – though tenuous – involvement with the Square Mile robberies, but also for the fact that he had taken bribes continuously over his fifteen-year career, unconcerned by any potential consequences, sheltered by the wing of the Brotherhood.

When Cuthbert gave evidence, he claimed that he was drunk at the time the recording was made, but this didn't hold up in trial. The still-unnamed-in-court Officer X responded with a written statement saying that all the allegations made by Cuthbert were totally unfounded, but that he was obliged to apologise for inaccurate evidence he had given in the case. On 20 July 1982, after a six-week trial, DS John Goldburn was sentenced to two years in prison. DCI Phillip Cuthbert was found guilty of taking up to £80,000 in bribes during his career: to secure bail, overlook past convictions, and not to gather evidence against the eight men who had been charged with the Williams & Glyn robbery. He was sentenced to three years.

On the tape recording, Cuthbert told Simmonds that Officer X was trying to make him a fall guy for Operation Countryman. In the mess of tangled ends that the investigation left behind, it seemed that someone had to be thrown to the lions: there were too many questions left unanswered. And even in its wake, there were too few answers for too many questions: the subject of police corruption highlighted by Countryman was taken up by Liberal Party MPs David Steel and Stephen Ross; and as late as March 1998, questions were asked in Parliament regarding the release of Countryman's findings. Even James Page's one-time rival John Alderson took up the cause, appearing on the same *World In Action* programme as Arthur Hambleton, despite being unconnected with the original investigation. In a strange turn of circumstance, Granada Television, the makers of that programme, had to pay out

£20,000 to a Metropolitan detective constable in 1985 because the officer had been caught on film exiting a police station while the programme's voice-over talked of CID officers taking bribes from criminals.

In the end, Operation Countryman highlighted the fact that, despite criminal proceeds dripping down to the lowest level, police corruption was the work of established, well-paid officers high in rank – the Officer Xs who flitted like blurred shapes through the investigation. One or a number of people, Officer X was not just the man above Phillip Cuthbert; he was also the man who warned James Page of 'Oates' and 'Tearle', themselves both Officer X . . .

The questions remain, such as: Why did Arthur Hambleton say in a statement that Countryman was *not* being obstructed and then go on *World In Action* two years later claiming that he issued the said statement knowing it was false? Or, did the Met and Director of Public Prosecutions force Countryman into submission? If 'Oates' left the force, was 'Tearle' the senior officer – Officer X – on the Regional Crime Squad, the mastermind of the Square Mile robberies? Was it a massive operation undertaken by police Freemasons? In fact, was the whole investigation instigated by Flying Squad Commander Don Neesham as a way of drawing attention away from criminal activities in his own division? The precise findings are still locked away in Home Office files, and from somewhere high up, Officer X looks down, untouchable.

BIBLIOGRAPHY

Paul Begg and Keith Skinner, *The Scotland Yard Files: 150 Years of the CID 1842–1992*, London: Headline, 1992.
Stephen Knight, *The Brotherhood: The Secret World of the Freemasons*, London: Granada, 1984.

Sir David McNee, *McNee's Law*, London: Collins, 1983.

James Morton, *Bent Coppers: A Survey of Police Corruption*, London: Warner Books, 1993.

Martin Short, *Inside The Brotherhood: Further Secrets of the Freemasons*, London: HarperCollins, 1993.

NOTES

1. Quoted in Sir David McNee, *McNee's Law*, London: Collins, 1983, p. 193.
2. Ibid., p. 194.
3. Martin Short, *Inside The Brotherhood: Further Secrets of the Freemasons*, London: HarperCollins, 1993, p. 293.
4. See Chapter 9, 'Operation Countryman' (pp. 86–96) in Stephen Knight's *The Brotherhood: The Secret World of the Freemansons*, London: Granada, 1984.
5. Quoted in Martin Short, *Inside The Brotherhood: Further Secrets of the Freemasons*, op. cit., pp. 295–6.
6. Ibid., p. 297.

3. LA NOIR: WHOSE LAW? A HISTORY OF THE LAPD

Chris Barber

The world was shocked when the savage beating of the helpless Rodney King by a gang of sadistic Los Angeles cops flashed across our TV screens. When a jury freed the lawmen responsible, it provoked mass riots on the city's streets, causing over fifty deaths and millions of dollars' worth of destruction. Recently LA's blue knights were at it again, providing another episode of this reality TV cop soap opera. But these events are merely a sitcom compared to what you didn't see. From its origins to today, the Los Angeles Police Department (LAPD) has been accused of sanctioning racist rednecks, brutal psychos and killer cops, achieving a reputation in law enforcement that could have been the pride and envy of Hitler's SS Storm Troopers.

LYNCH-MOB JUSTICE: LAPD 1850–1899[1]

At the end of the Mexico–USA war, Mexico ceded vast areas of land to the USA, including the state of California. The Gold Rush caused thousands of crazy prospectors to 'go west' to the Pacific state; and the pueblo (town) of Los Angeles was declared a 'City' (of Angels) in 1850, with 1,610 citizens.

The Los Angeles Rangers was the city's first Police Department, founded by Dr AW Hope in 1853, in response to the murder of a City Marshall. Their uniform consisted of a white ribbon, but the 'Los Angeles City Guards' soon replaced them.

From the outset, LA law was dispensed inauspiciously by mob rule. In 1854, LA Mayor Stephen C Foster led a rambunctious mob of vigilantes, who busted a suspect from a makeshift prison and lynched him.

In the absence of a formal prison, convicts were chained to logs in a yard. A jail was considered less important than enforcing statutory racism, enshrined by the Supreme Court in 1850, stating:

> *No black or mulatto person, or Indian, shall be permitted to give evidence in favour of, or against any white person. Every person who shall have one-eighth part or more of Negro blood shall be deemed a mulatto and every person who shall have one-half of Indian blood shall be deemed Indian.*

They forgot to include Asians, but amended this oversight shortly thereafter.

LA was a lawless, Wild West frontier town, brimming with casinos and saloons. When Sheriff James Barton was killed in 1857, suspects were arbitrarily rounded up and eleven were sent to the gallows.

By 1869, the city's population had increased to 5,614, patronising 285 businesses (110 being saloons). The ramshackle of Bible-bashing peacekeepers, community vigilantes and rent-a-mob citizenry, was finally organised into a professional cop-squad. City Marshall William C Warren established a police headquarters, employing six officers, paid for by civic fines and tariffs. The Marshall served as tax collector and dogcatcher, and was personally awarded two-and-a-half per cent of duties he collected.

Old habits die hard and, despite this reorganisation, mob law continued to control the streets. One day alone in 1871, an angry posse, uninterrupted by law officers, lynched nineteen Chinese migrants. When eight suspects were eventually arrested for the hangings they were imprisoned in San Quentin, but released less than two years later.

From 1875 until 1916, horseback patrols were deployed on city streets. Yet the City Marshall remained unable to impose discipline on subordinates; one Marshall was even shot dead by his men. This provoked the City Council to orchestrate a massive shake-up, intent on instilling discipline. The first Board of Police Commissioners was established, electing Jacob T Gerkins as chief in 1876. A regulation uniform was made compulsory – a blue serge jacket and felt cap. Additionally, officers themselves had to pay $6 each for a silver, eight-point badge.

Between 1876 and 1889, thirteen new chiefs came and went. The earliest traffic squad hit the streets under Chief George E Gard in 1881, to control 'horse, wagon and carriage' chaos. In 1886, Robert William Stewart and Roy Green were the first two African Americans to join the force, then numbering eighteen officers.

RED ALERT: LAPD 1900–1920[2]

John M Glass served eleven years as chief, from 1889. He moved the Central Station Headquarters to West 1st Street, where it remained for sixty years. Glass also augmented the first entry-level standards for tyros.

At the beginning of the twentieth century, the population of LA had grown to 100,000, policed by only seventy cops, who struggled to control rampant crime and traffic chaos. Now local politicians and their cronies (civil servants) started to meddle with the control of the police force (an intrusion which has compromised the LAPD ever since). From the mayor's office through to council planners, for the sake of expedient vote catching, city development dealings or more blatant corruption, civic policing served partisan interests.

Up to 1923, sixteen incumbent chiefs were appointed and sacked, according to changing political regimes; police personnel increased to two hundred. Over the same period, the city was transformed into a modern, urban environment. This was accompanied by much industrial strife, as labour unions organised against fat-cat bosses.

The *Los Angeles Times* was the city's most popular and influential newspaper. It ceaselessly propagated campaigns against trades unions and advocated scabbing during strikes. In 1910, the paper's own employees engaged in a protracted strike and on 1 October, the *Los Angeles Times* building was blown up with dynamite. Several union activists were arrested and imprisoned.

Chief Charles E Sebastian ran the Department from 1911 to 1915, subsequently becoming the first former LAPD member to be elected as mayor (for his harsh crusade against vice). Clarence E Snively succeeded him as police chief. Snively declared that cigarette smoking caused 'weak bodies' and 'weak morals', being the major contributor to youth delinquency. He funded the 'Anti-Cigarette Clinic' to discourage juveniles from smoking. A year later, Snively and his ideas went up in smoke (replaced by a further eight chiefs up to 1923).

When the United States entered the First World War, the LAPD was determined not to miss out on the action. Attention was concentrated on tackling violation of federal offences, such as 'failure to register as a German Alien enemy' and 'seditious utterances'. But Europe's fermenting communist revolutions were perceived as the main threat, so the Department set up the War Squad to counter subversive activities. Striking workers were labelled 'Reds' and frequently subjected to intimidating investigations by the police.

Reacting to an upsurge in violent late-night street crime, the LAPD Flying Squad formed in 1918, equipped with a couple of fast cars. However, by 1920, corruption was endemic throughout local government and its police department.

ROTTEN TO THE CORE: LAPD 1920–1925[3]

Prohibition took its toll on LA; bootleggers and gangsters dominated the city's business community, protected by bent politicians and cops. High-ranking city officials could pull strings, effectively putting interested parties beyond the law. Booze, vice and gambling, created a huge black market economy, overlorded by multi-millionaire hoodlums who bribed elected officials and top cops. In one fifteen-month period, over 100 of LAPD's 1,200 officers were forced out over misconduct. Black market bosses also established legitimate business fronts, using cops to break strikes and smash picket lines.

By 1922, the LA populace hit 1 million, inhabiting an area covering 363 square miles. Police chiefs were selected by elected city officials, eager to repay favours and election donations from local entrepreneurs. Businessmen had specific concerns about how policing and the law might best protect their interests, favouring police chiefs who could be counted on to 'turn a blind eye' to certain trading practices, or provide an advance tip-off prior to police operations. Rewarded and protected by their 'friends' in city hall, these top-dog cops remain in power so long as they don't rock the boat or attract unwanted attention . . . or at least until the next city elections.

The gravy train spread pay-offs throughout the ranks (diminishing in value) offering tax-free 'perks' to the lowliest foot patrols. So the turnover of the Department's manpower was dramatic as the rot deepened. Protecting specific business interests became indistinguishable from policing the whole community. In 1921, LAPD arrested Upton Sinclair for reading the US Declaration of Independence in public!

During the early 1920s only one of the many passing police chiefs attempted to stop the rot. He was August Vollmer, former Chief of Berkeley, California, Police. He accepted the position only for one year, his appointment secretly sanctioned by underworld bosses, hoping to quell the mounting protestations and alarm generated by the media. Vollmer overhauled the Department, improving professional standards and working conditions, and establishing the Scientific Investigation Division.

In retrospect it seems a perniciously ironic cliché, but it was Vollmer who first stated: 'There is no higher calling than that of a policeman. I would rather be a policeman than President.' Significantly for policing around the world, Vollmer instigated the 'Crime Crushers Division' (now Metropolitan Division), starting with 300 officers, which calibrated available police resources on districts with the highest crime rates.

It was the LAPD's year of permanent revolution, until politics and corruption crept back.

GUN LAW: LAPD 1926–1949[4]

After the virtual destruction of Europe in the First World War, the LA suburb of Hollywood had become the world's biggest film production factory. Migrant workers from across the US, and Mexican immigrants, poured into LA throughout the 1920/30s, seduced by the silver screen or struggling to escape economic depression. They were soon awakened from their dreams, forced into squalid, overcrowded urban ghettos, jobless or underpaid and overworked, struggling to survive, many forced into crime.

James E Davis replaced Vollmer at the helm in 1926, initiating his comic-strip notion of gun law with his fifty-man strong 'Gun Squad'. Davis announced: 'Hold court on gunmen in the Los Angeles streets; I want them brought in dead, not alive, and will reprimand any officer who shows the least mercy to a criminal.'

Under Chief Davis, LAPD officers were rigorously trained as marksmen and firearms experts. He also implemented the dragnet strategy for hunting down elusive criminals, and stressed the potential of statistical analysis to calculate criminal trends. Top cop Davis sacked 240 officers for 'bad conduct'.

Chief Roy E Steckel got off to a flying start in 1931, forming an air patrol of ten officers in a fixed-wing squadron. But citizens had completely lost faith in their police force. Mayor John C Porter (1929–1933) tried to restore public confidence by hiring former officers as private detectives, to spy on the city's administration and police department, to bust corrupt officials. They were pejoratively known as 'super snoops' to cops, and the scheme was dropped after three years.

Steckel had more success, introducing 'the most modern municipal radio system in the world', in 1931. From eight permanently manned switchboards and a transmitter in Elysian Park, citizens' emergency calls were broadcast directly to cops, manning 44 patrol cars. Using the call code KGFL, they achieved a response time of three minutes anywhere in the city.

In 1933, Davis bounced back as chief. This time around he manipulated anti-communist paranoia, immediately forming the 'Red Squad' to 'investigate and control radical activities, strikes, and riots'. Fully supported by local government and business, the squad harassed and intimidated any citizen they deemed to be subversive, one police commissioner boasting: 'The more the police beat them up and wreck their head-quarters, the better. Communists have no constitutional rights and I won't listen to anyone who defends them.'

Paranoia over the rising influx of illegal aliens caused another panic the LAPD took very seriously. A border patrol comprising 126 officers was created, to uphold new state law prohibiting people unable to support themselves from entry. Police picket boats vigilantly patrolled LA's harbour.

When Frank L Shaw won a term as mayor, he appointed his brother Joe to overall control of the Police and Fire Departments. Public disenchantment in law enforcement plummeted to new depths, until Shaw was ousted in 1938.

The incumbent Mayor Bowron finally mounted a massive clean-up operation, forcing dozens of corrupt city commissioners into early retirement. Thereafter, 45 high-ranking police officers summarily 'resigned', for failing to correct their 'questionable practices'. In 1939, Arthur C Hohmann was appointed chief, charged to modernise organisation throughout the force.

The war effort depleted LAPD manpower in the early 1940s, while foot patrols were assigned to guard the harbour and watch for enemy submarines. In 1943, the police failed to curtail the 'zoot suit' riots which raged for four days. This violent street gang war began when groups of racist American sailors attacked east LA's Mexican–American community (whose gang members wore zoot suits). The conflict resulted in hundreds of serious injuries.

CHIEF PARKER: LAPD 1950–1966

LAPD's most renowned and admired chief was William H Parker, who took control in 1950 and retained the position for sixteen years. The Department's administration headquarters situated on North Los Angeles Street is named Parker Centre after him. He was a stickler for the rules, intolerant of corruption in his force, imposed strict discipline on the rank and file, and made the police more accountable to public scrutiny.

Parker was more successful in modernising and cleaning up the Department than any of his predecessors; although reactionary and intolerant, he was worshiped by his officers and popular with the general public. However, if you were black, manifested liberal tendencies or used drugs, beware if you attracted police attention:

Since the days of the legendary Chief William Parker in the early 1950s, the LAPD has been regarded by L.A.'s Black community as a redneck army of occupation.[5]

The previous decade's 'zoot suit' riots set an alarming precedent, which flourished in the LAPD under Chief Parker. White Americans wearing official US military uniforms perpetrated violent racially motivated attacks on LA's ghetto-based Mexican–American community. In the aftermath, there was no official apology for Mexicans or disciplinary action against military personnel. That amounts to official US/LAPD sanction of actions by white supremacists (recalling the German Nazi government's disenfranchisement of Jews and state-sanctioned attacks on pogroms by the uniformed nationalist SS). By the 1950s, LA was home to large black and Mexican communities. They inhabited poverty-stricken and overcrowded ghettos, the worst conditions in the city. While there was a long tradition of racial prejudice in the

LAPD, this was largely expressed in isolated incidents, without official state approval. That changed under Chief Parker, whose outspoken tirades against blacks and defence of storm-trooper policing in ghettos amounted to institutional racism:

> The black gangs of the 1950s also had to confront the implacable (often lethal) racism of Chief Parker's LAPD ... The policing of the ghetto was becoming simultaneously less corrupt but more militarised and brutal. Under previous police chiefs, for example, Central Avenue's boisterous, interracial night scene had simply been shaken down for tribute; under Parker – a puritanical crusader against 'race-mixing' – nightclubs and juke joints were raided and shuttered.[6]

John Dolphin owned a successful R&B record label in the city's black business neighbourhood. In 1954 he led a protest supported by 150 black business representatives against the 'campaign of intimidation and terror',[7] organised by Newton Division LAPD, to undermine interracial trade. Dolphin claimed officers blockaded stores, warning customers 'it was too dangerous to hang around black neighbourhoods'.

Parker's outspoken and unapologetic racism was one aspect of his overall worldview; a simplistic hodgepodge of reactionary perspectives, propped up by people's territorial readiness to expect the worst and presume anything lacking familiarity is a threat. 'The Communists furthered the heroin and marijuana trade, because drug use sped the moral degeneration of America,'[8] claimed Parker. He used his friends in the press (particularly the *Herald Express*) to call for the border with Mexico to be closed, and tacitly supported a campaign demanding the execution of drug dealers.

Honesty was not among his virtues. He falsified crime statistics to lend support to a campaign against council housing, creating the illusion that low-rent housing estates reflected 'jungle life'[9] and were harbingers of crime. His populist appeal to the public served to strengthen his own power base.

Further, Chief Parker testified before a US Commission on Civil Rights in 1960, that his 'blue-line' (LAPD) were the real 'embattled minority',[10] all that protected American community values from the growing crime deluge lurking in black ghettos (manipulating public panic so City Hall wouldn't force financial cuts on the Police Department). Social rehabilitation projects were also targeted by Parker, blacks and Chicanos being innately 'hardcore' criminals, incapable of reform and destined to live out their existence in state prisons.

CALLING ALL CARS!

One black victim of Parker's LAPD was George Jackson, who records his ruthless arrest by cops in *Soledad Brother*, his collected prison letters:

I was 15, and full grown (I haven't grown an inch since then). A cop shot me six times point-blank on that job, as I was standing with my hands in the air. After the second shot, when I was certain that he was trying to murder me, I charged him. His gun was empty and he only hit me twice by the time I had closed with him – 'Oh, get this wild nigger off me.' . . .

Since all blacks are thought of as rats the third degree started before I was taken to hospital. Medical treatment was offered as a reward for cooperation. At first they didn't know I had been hit, but as soon as they saw the blood running from my sleeve, the

*questions began. A bullet had passed through my
forearm, another had sliced my leg. I sat in the back of
the pig car and bled for two hours before they were
convinced that lockjaw must have set in already.*[11]

In response to the rapid growth of black radical Muslim
groups, Parker shifted his attention from black street
gangs to black militants, as representing the biggest
threat. In 1962, LAPD officers engaged in an unprovoked attack on a Nation of Islam mosque in South-
Central. A Muslim was shot dead by cops and six were
injured.

A significant event occurred in 1965 – the Watts
Rebellion. Juvenile black street gangs had evolved since
the late 1940s, to protect black kids from racist white
gangs. Black gangs marked their turfs, based around
local schools. (By contrast, Chicano gangs established
turfs around neighbouring territories.) Notorious gangs
from the black South-Central ghetto included the
Businessmen, Gladiators and Slausons. In the 1950s,
feuds developed within the black community. By the
early 1960s, rumbles between black gangs were commonplace, as ghettos got more overcrowded and dilapi-
dated, wage differentials between black and white
workers drastically increased, and the number of jobless
blacks rose dramatically. Meanwhile LAPD storm-
trooper tactics relentlessly oppressed the ghettos, fuelling tensions.

Something had to crack and finally it happened: long-
feuding black gangs suddenly forgot their differences to
unite against the police. An estimated 75,000 people
took to the streets to kick the LAPD out of the ghetto.
Even with back-up from the National Guard, the blue
line could not handle the onslaught and were forced to
retreat.

A furious Chief Parker berated the rioters. One of Parker's keenest supporters was Cardinal McIntyre, an austerely conservative Catholic, racist, anti-communist and anti-liberal. When some newspapers suggested police had provoked the rebellion, the Cardinal (one of LA's most powerful and influential clergy) publicly defended Parker's policing methods, describing rebels as 'inhuman, almost bestial'. His pontificating angered neighbouring parishioners, some with largely black congregations, causing an acrimonious split in the city's Catholic Church.

About a year later, Chief Parker suffered a fatal heart attack (1966).

INTERIM COPS: LAPD 1967–1978

Deputy Chief Thad F Brown assumed interim command, pending the appointment of Thomas Reddin in 1967. The Department made the headlines again that year, when officers in riot gear attacked a peaceful anti-Vietnam-war demo at Century City, leaving many injuries. Determination to control the counter-culture gatherings around Elysian Park increased and Griffith apparently caused police even to break up family picnics. Reddin retired shortly thereafter, replaced by Roger E Murdock, subsequently handing over to Chief Edward M Davis.

Ed Davis focused attention on community relations, forming the first Neighbourhood Watch programmes as well as going to the dogs with the K-9 Corps. From 1974, the School Buy Program began, with undercover officers attending high schools posing as students wanting to buy drugs, to entrap potential dealers. In 1975 he augmented the Department's Asian Task Force to police the growing Asian community; additionally Davis decentralised the Office of Operations. The changing emphasis in the early 1970s, towards spying and entrapment policing, perhaps attempts to counter alternative crime trends . . .

In the aftermath of the Watts rebellion, brotherhood in the ghetto held firm, strengthening solidarity for the black liberation movement. The building momentum and radicalisation of black youth inspired formation of the Black Panther Party (largely from former street gang punks). The Panthers saw the LAPD as the enemy and prepared for war, planning a militant underground tactical strategy for the struggle. They also supported less clandestine manoeuvres, like an attempt by the Black Congress and People's Tribunal to put LAPD on trial for murdering Gregory Clark. LAPD co-ordinated its response with the FBI, engaging a covert campaign utilising state-of-the-art surveillance technology.

When Panther leaders Carter and Huggins were assassinated in 1969 (apparently by rival black militants) the Panthers drifted into disarray. Although never proven, it is widely believed LAPD/FBI involvement was responsible for the deaths. Certainly LAPD's Public Disorder Intelligence Division co-operated with the debut of SWAT teams in a day-long siege of the Panther's South-Central headquarters.

It's no fluke that the decline of Panther power in the early 1970s coincided with the re-emergence of LA gangs, first-generation Crips or OGs (Original Gangsters) hitting the streets in their low-hip baggy trousers and regimental colours.

Davis retired in 1978,[12] replaced by Assistant Chief Robert F Rock, pending the appointment of Daryl F Gates the same year.

THE GREAT GATES: 1978–1992

A protégé of Chief Parker, outspoken self-publicist and staunch advocate of confrontational policing, Chief Gates retained the esteem of both his cops and the general public; second only in trumped-up stature to Parker's own mythical status. Gates wasted no time in launching headline-grabbing stunts, demanding the USA invade Colombia, and offering President Jimmy Carter SWAT squads to rescue hostages from Iran.

Meanwhile another attention-grabbing, white ex-cop, with five-years' service in 77th Street's 'Fort Apache', and now known as 'Masked Marvel':

> Appeared in disguise on a series of local television shows to luridly chronicle the pathological racism and trigger-happiness of the 'blue knights' towards ordinary Blacks. Gates . . . ridiculed these charges and the 'liberals' who listened to them. Soon afterwards came the police killing of Eulia Love, a 39-year-old Black widow in default of her gas bill. As Gates defended the twelve 38-caliber holes in Mrs. Love's body before a cowed Police Commission . . . [Protestors] asked the Justice Department to probe a pattern of systematic abuse of non-whites, including 'more than 300 police shootings of minority citizens in the last decade'. Meanwhile, the Coalition Against Police Abuse (CAPA) collected tens of thousands of signatures calling for the establishment of a civilian police review board.[13]

Despite calls for his resignation, Chief Gates survived the debacle, protected by his political alliance with Mayor Bradley:

> Chief Gates was only emboldened to taunt the Black community with increasingly contemptuous or absurd

excuses for police brutality. In 1982, for example,
following a rash of LAPD 'chokehold' killings of young
Black men in custody, he advocated the extraordinary
theory that the deaths were the fault of the victims'
racial anatomy, not excessive police force: 'We may be
finding that in some blacks when [the carotid
chokehold] is applied the veins or arteries do not open
as fast as they do on normal people.'[14]

As Police Chief throughout ex-LA Congressman Reagan's presidency, Gates implemented Proposition 13,
overseeing cutbacks in the Department's budget and
manpower. Community-based crime-stopper schemes
were strengthened; cutting-edge radio communications
and crime prevention technology were introduced, and
routine tasks passed to expanding civil personnel or
voluntary service sections. Manpower was axed to 6,900
by 1985 (when New York employed 28,700 police
personnel).

In 1984 the city hosted the XXIII Summer Olympic
Games, prompting Gates to boast:

History has recorded no other Olympaid when so much
was demanded of the police department . . . It was a
monumental undertaking . . . And this is what
happened: Not a single act of terrorism occurred. Not
one![15]

Having pioneered Special Weapons and Tactics (SWAT)
teams in 1972, Gates strengthened and increased their
operations while chief, and he implemented Drug Abuse
Resistance Education (DARE). DARE targeted attention
on developing youth resistance to narcotics, based on
the premise that the older generation had already lost
the struggle. (Perhaps the ageing chief based his con-

clusion on experience; although it was his son who later compromised the old man's public image, when he was arrested for holding up a chemist at gunpoint and demanding drugs!)

From the late 1980s, crack cocaine hit the streets, fuelling a dramatic increase in violent crime. Chief Gates claimed the city was besieged by a 'deadly plague', orchestrated by dual out-of-control crime epidemics: drug trafficking and street gang violence. Most murders and bank robberies were apparently drug related; 200 street gangs and 10 motorbike chapters were blamed for inner-city crime.

As usual, it was the deprived black ghettos like South-Central that took the brunt of the latest crime wave and new generation of street gangs. The panic caused black community spokespeople to call for police protection, supporting the enforcement of dusk-till-dawn youth curfews in non-white districts. Chief Gates leapt at the opportunity to bring former critics into his fan club:

> With an eye for media exposure, the Chief launched the first of his heavily hyped anti-gang sweeps. (The LAPD already conducted regular sweeps to drive homeless people off the streets of Downtown.) This so-called Gang Related Active Trafficker Suppression program (GRATS) targeted 'drug-neighbourhoods' for raids by 200–300 police under orders to 'stop and interrogate anyone who they suspect is a gang member, basing their assumptions on their dress or their use of gang hand signals'. Thus, on the flimsy 'probable cause' of red shoelaces or high-five handshakes, the taskforces in February and March [1987] mounted nine sweeps, impounded five hundred cars and made nearly fifteen hundred arrests.[16]

Determined to catch the media spotlight in the aftermath, Chief Gates made a self-congratulatory speech, claiming the LAPD had won the war on crime in South-Central. Some hours later, 'Crips' and 'Bloods' (the most infamous of LA's street gangs) had a gunfight on a crowded street in a posh neighbourhood, accidentally killing a nineteen-year-old woman.

HAMMER HORROR

As the shit hit the fan, Chief Gates insisted that the LAPD was in control of the situation, announcing the launch of Operation Hammer, utilising all the Department's reserve manpower in 'super-sweeps'. (According to the *Herald Examiner*, 14 January 1990, a retiring, high-ranking LAPD officer claimed Hammer was 'a hokey publicity deal' they had scrambled together.) Hammer's debut performance featured a spectacular, 1,000-strong cast of patrolmen, with additional special back-up units waiting in the wings. They were let loose on a ten-square-mile area of South-Central, making 1,453 arrests, mainly black kids for minor offences, forced to lie on the pavement or spreadeagled against walls at gunpoint. Most of this body count weren't charged at all, but were searched and questioned, their personal details being entered into the LAPD's new super-computer, for future use.

On the streets, black citizens were largely uncooperative, with LAPD trampling over their basic human rights, despite black community representatives supporting Gates. One LAPD official winged: 'People in the neighbourhood instead of being on our side, make all kinds of accusations.'[17] Black citizens alleged police making Hammer raids actually provoked an escalation in gang warfare, by defacing gang graffiti logos to look like rival gangs attacked it; or picking up gang suspects and dumping them on enemy turf. The police commission registered a record number of official complaints against the police.

Back in 1986, Gates publicly vilified Community Youth Gang Services (CYGS) for attempting to draw warring gangs into a truce. Low-level street crime and social reforms were not going to win an increase in LAPD's budget or consolidate power for Gates.

On 5 April 1988, cops shot dead an unarmed teenager as he crouched in terror behind an Adams Boulevard palm tree. Police alleged the suspected gang member had reached into his trousers, so they opened fire! The Department claimed Hammer busted 500 crack dens in 1988. Another victim was an 81-year-old retired builder, knocked down by a hail of police bullets while (according to his niece) he held his hands up; no drugs were discovered in his pad. LAPD claimed elderly pensioners were being paid to let dealers use their flats as drug shops. Neither case attracted much media attention, nor was any disciplinary action taken against the cops involved.

The southern California branch of the American Civil Liberties Union (ACLU), which had regularly been under LAPD surveillance over the years, launched a campaign against Hammer. It failed to attract much attention and was soon abandoned in favour of other issues. A group of concerned solicitors collected statements from Hammer harassment victims, to build a case against the police. But when a once prominent civil rights activist cast aspersions about their political affiliations, they abandoned the case.

Even Chief Gates admitted things 'got out of hand'[18] when 88 Southwest Division (a precinct already in turmoil over complaints by black officers about internal racism) raided flats at 3900 Dalton Street in August

1988. The squad busted into apartments with sledgehammers, tooled-up with shotguns and waving search warrants. There followed (what residents later called) 'an orgy of violence', cops spray-painting walls with 'LAPD Rules' while kicking and punching residents. Furniture and walls were smashed up, staircases dismantled, washing machines chucked into bathtubs, bleach poured over clothes . . . (The Red Cross was so appalled by the destruction left by cops that they offered emergency aid and shelter to residents.)

Thirty-two people were rounded up during the blitz and bundled off to the precinct. There they were punched and assaulted with long-handle torches, even ordered to whistle marching tunes. Finally, just two kids were charged for possession of small quantities of dope; neither kid lived on the block and no wanted gang members or weapons were found.

For once, an internal investigation into police action was unavoidable. The FBI was pursuing complaints of civil rights violations and while dozens of witness statements were verified, accounts by cops proved unsustainable. LAPD took criminal or disciplinary action against 38 officers (including Captain Thomas Elfmont who ordered his officers to 'make uninhabitable'[19] apartments searched).

For a few months, Chief Gates kept a low public profile as Hammer operations continued. However, he couldn't keep his head down for long, bouncing back into controversy when called to testify in another case contending police brutality. The Larezes – a Chicano family – filed charges against police raiders for malicious assault. Gates told reporters that 'Mr Larez was lucky to have only his nose broken'.[20] His remark so enraged the jury on the trial that they raised the victims' damages by $200,000 and ordered Chief Gates to pay up himself (an unprecedented request). After a cooling-off period, the City Council paid the cash, at Mayor Bradley's request, along with $3 million in compensation for the Dalton Street fiasco.

The show must go on, and in a crack-house raid off Main Street in April 1989, an all-star cast, including former president's wife Nancy Reagan and Chief Gates himself, joined in the encore. After a SWAT team had removed all weapons from the premises, with the occupants lying face-down on the floor, the celebrity couple toured the ramshackle apartment, Nancy dazzling the assembled media army in her shimmering LAPD flak-jacket.

By 1990, the full results of Operation Hammer were open to scrutiny and astoundingly poor. Most of the catch comprised motoring offences, drunks and teenage curfew breakers (dusk-to-dawn curfews were imposed on teenagers in black districts as part of the operation). Fifty thousand suspects had been pulled in by police (the total youth population of LA amounting to only 100,000!) Nine out of ten suspects were released without charge. (There was one 'benefit', the reversal of the Department's financial restraints saw the total government budget exceed $419,500,000: employing 7,200 uniformed and 2,500 civil staff.)[21]

The chief's response was astonishing, if predictable; he proposed stepping up and institutionalising sweeps in 'narcotic enforcement zones'. Further, Gates suggested gang members be interned in prison camps, surrounded by minefields (got to catch them first!).

KING OF THE COPS

With his retirement looming, Chief Gates had created a powder keg waiting to explode. And in 1991, it did:

*Okay, so the nation has 'recovered' from the
death-dealing riots spawned by the ludicrous, racially
inspired verdict in which four white cops were found
not guilty of the videotaped beating of Rodney King in
Los Angeles . . . Police brutality finally is out of the
closet . . . The quartet of 'LA's finest' that kicked,
stomped, shocked and clubbed the defenceless
25-year-old black man – 56 times in 81 seconds as a
dozen other cops watched – demonstrated for white
America what black America always has known: that
police brutality is alive and well in the land.*[22]

Amidst over 50 deaths, smoke clouds still bellowing
from the burning ghetto, Chief Willie L Williams
assumed command, as LAPD's 50th (but first Afro-
American) chief in 1992. He came with a $607,000
grant from the Department of Justice to reform the
LAPD, based on recommendations of the Christopher
Commission (inquiry into the Rodney King fiasco). This
was spent providing new stations, cars and facilities,
along with a new training programme for recruits.

RAMPART RAP: LAPD's NAUGHTY NINETIES[23]
In October 1996, LAPD officers Rafael Perez and Nino
Durden shot Javier Francisco Ovando four times in the
neck and chest during a covert police surveillance
operation monitoring drug-dealing street gangs. A
month later the hearing commenced in a Los Angeles
County Hall of Justice courtroom. Durden and Perez
alleged Ovando had assaulted them with a Tec-22
semi-automatic handgun. Honduran-born Ovando was
wheeled into court, wizened and emaciated – paralysed
from the waist down since the event, barely able to talk
and accompanied by his public defender, Tamar Toister.
Ovando spoke no English, necessitating an interpreter;

he asserted his innocence of the charge, claiming 'bad cops' tried to kill him.

The court was informed nineteen-year-old Ovando had '18' tattooed on his neck, signifying membership of LA's 18th Street Gang, notorious for ruthless killings and drug pushing. A jury was not going to believe Ovando (who had no criminal record) against front-line police officers. The crime scene was a dark, derelict, upper-storey room overlooking a street and alleyway known for drug dealing. Durden and Perez frequented the room to surreptitiously monitor the street, and claimed to be surprised when an armed man entered from the illuminated hall behind them. Perez testified they turned around sharpish, firing first, as Ovando hit the deck in a pool of blood. When back-up arrived, they were amazed he was still alive.

Based only on Perez's account and the prosecution hypothesis that Ovando was a cop-killing gang assassin, he was sentenced to 23 years' incarceration. But this apparently clear-cut case would lead to the LAPD's worst ever scandal: investigations into the conduct of 70 officers (20 were sacked), cops being jailed, release of a hundred framed prisoners, and the LAPD was put under federal government supervision.

The officers concerned belonged to LAPD's Crash *crack*-elite, of Rampart Division. West of Normandie Avenue and Downtown, South of Sunset Boulevard, Rampart is the most overcrowded district in the western USA and top of the LA chart for murder and drug dealing. Amidst eight square miles of high-rise blocks and derelict buildings, the highest concentration of illegal immigrants survives. Since the early 1980s, about 60 gangs have controlled the area; designating it the main target area of the discredited Crash and Hammer initiatives.

Officer Rafael Perez was born in Puerto Rico in 1967. Still a child when he emmigrated to the United States, he settled in Philadelphia with his mother. His lawyer claimed Perez longed to be a cop since his childhood and vividly recollected hanging out on street corners, watching drug-pushers and dreaming of arresting them. In 1985, Perez graduated from high school and enlisted in the Marines. He joined LAPD in 1989. Following a spell as a routine patrolman, he was assigned to a drugs unit, transferring to Rampart Crash in 1995. Speaking fluent Spanish was considered a big asset to the force (many Rampart inhabitants can't speak English) and he soon distinguished himself as a ruthless crime fighter with street cred.

Despite its critics, Crash survived post-Gates:

Crash officers worked in tough places and were expected to confront violence with violence. Rampart Crash, which varied in size from a dozen officers in winter to as many as 20 in summer, when gang activity peaked, was an especially tight-knit group. Officers gave plaques to comrades who shot gang members. Rampart members wore logos and patches, the most notorious of which was a skull with a cowboy hat and a poker hand of a pair of aces and a pair of eights, the dead man's hand that the frontier outlaw Wild Bill Hickock was holding when he was shot to death. 'Rampart was home to a bunch of cowboy cops,' said David Smith, an LAPD captain who had several encounters with them . . .

Captain Smith recounted that when he responded to a call from a Rampart resident who had been roughed up by police officers, he was told to mind his own business.[24]

Due to overcrowding at the station, Rampart Crash moved to a separate headquarters three kilometres away in 1995. From here they operated by their own rules, free from scrutiny; they even changed their station key code from 999 (common to all LAPD stations) to 888, rejecting the standard issue entrance key given to all officers. Rampart Crash further enforced their independence by refusing to wear the required cop uniform, always dressing street-wise.

So Rampart Crash became the new gang on the block, tooled-up to rumble Bloods or Crips and their numerous offshoot street gangs. But unlike their neighbourhood rivals, these guys were above the Law, loyal only to themselves and their sectarian jungle code. Perez was a hard-boiled initiate, with a gang-busting record that impressed Crash comrades.

There was an alternative version of the Ovando shooting, largely corroborated by his (then) pregnant girlfriend Valensuela and involving his pal Nene (subsequently missing). Accordingly Nene and Ovando were homeless, sleeping in the trash-strewn building when apprehended by the cop duo. They were handcuffed and brutally interrogated about a recent gang heist. Then Nene was released and scampered, bumping into Valensuela on the stairs. While talking, they heard shots from upstairs and hastily departed . . .

BLUE-LINE ON WHITE-LINES[25]

With Ovando long off the streets, life in Rampart continued as normal: street-gang massacres and drug-crazed homicides, all under the jack-boot occupation and controlling gaze of LAPD's Crash troops. In November 1997, two armed bandits robbed the Bank of America in South-Central. Customer service manager Errolyn Romero handed over $722,000. Detectives interviewing her discovered she had ordered extra cash earlier that day. Under interrogation she broke down, revealing one of the robbers was her boyfriend, David Mack, a cop who served in Rampart.

Mack was a close friend of Perez and investigators discovered they went to Las Vegas together after the hold-up. They were soon picked up, but Perez was released, claiming he knew nothing about the bank job. Yet they had worked together for years; Perez said Mack once saved his life by shooting an armed drug-pusher they were searching (other accounts claim the pusher was unarmed). Mack was sentenced to 14 years, but the stolen cash was never recovered. Detectives believed Perez drove the getaway car but couldn't prove it.

Another incident attracted attention to the Perez gang in February 1998. A Rampart Crash team arrested a young suspect, holding him in their cop-den interview room. Officer Brian Hewitt entered, beating up and choking the detainee until he vomited blood. Upon his release, the prisoner checked into hospital and the assault was reported. Hewitt and another officer were sacked; a third officer was reprimanded.

A few weeks later, LAPD's property unit (responsible for safeguarding evidence for court) handed out six pounds of cocaine from a recent bust, to an officer involved. The evidence was never returned and had been signed out to a bogus name. Officer Rafael Perez's name had cropped up in association with all these incidents. Further, it was discovered that Perez regularly checked out quantities of cocaine that weren't returned, sometimes on cases that didn't concern him. A full-scale, top-secret internal investigation was ordered.

With several years' LAPD service, Perez was no stranger to official procedures in the force. But, having eluded detection for so long, it must have gone to his head. After shadowing him for weeks while gathering evidence, his house was surrounded by a convoy of police cars, lights flashing and sirens screeching. Perez was handcuffed and taken away, while shocked neighbours told police they thought he was a wealthy property speculator. The full-time cop had recently renovated his luxurious apartment; no expense spared (well beyond his $58,000 base salary). Charged with possession and sale of cocaine, grand theft and forgery, he was tried in December 1998. The jury returned a deadlocked verdict, eight-to-four for conviction, necessitating a retrial.

Investigators consolidated their case against Perez, discovering dozens of undisclosed credits in his bank account, dating back years. Perez was married and had a young daughter. His wife was also a civil employee of LAPD. Detectives got tough, threatening Perez with charges against his wife if he didn't come clean. Recently appointed LAPD Chief Parks was driving to out police misconduct.

Faced with the threat to involve his wife, both possibly facing long jail sentences, Perez consulted his solicitor Winston Kevin McKesson, to negotiate a deal with prosecutors. Finally, in September 1999, an agreement was reached. Perez would blow the lid on years of Rampart Crash misconduct; in return he wanted a five-year sentence in a secure jail, immunity from further prosecution and total immunity for his wife. District Attorney Garcetti was reluctant; the prisoner might be released in less than two years on that deal. However, Perez added that an innocent man was serving his third year, of a 23-year sentence. Was the prosecutor prepared to let him rot? Deal accepted. So Perez started talking through 50 hours of intense interrogation by LAPD detectives.

Regarding the cocaine thefts, Perez stated he began dealing in 1997, after he and Durden arrested a gang member carrying a pound of cocaine. The suspect also had a pager, which the cops kept (as well as the cocaine). Via a pager call, Perez (posing as a dealer) arranged to sell a quarter-pound of the narcotic. Perez claimed they intended to arrest the customer, but Durden suggested: ' "Screw it. Let's just sell to him." And I completely agreed.'

Two more deals were struck using the pager, the cops receiving $10,000. It all seemed too easy so Perez decided the police's own stash shouldn't be wasted. He admitted to stealing eight pounds (police reckon far more was involved, but settled for this).

RAMPART BLUES[26]

'These guys don't play by the rules; we don't have to play by the rules,' Perez explained. 'When I planted a case on someone, did I feel bad? Not once. I felt good. I felt, you know, I'm taking this guy off the streets.'

Rampart Crash tactics were approved by Sgt. Edward Ortiz, Perez's commander. 'Ortiz had the final say-so on everything.' Framing gang members on narcotics or weapon charges was common practice. A case in point was Rafael Zambrano, attending a gang party that was suddenly busted by party-Crash-ers. Everyone was ordered to kneel while Officer Brian Hewitt marched up and down, selecting people at whim and telling officers what to charge them with. Zambrano landed gun possession. Despite being unarmed, he pleaded guilty for a shorter sentence and served 16 months.

Crash officers were always prepared for a quick fix-up, keeping their own stash of guns, taken from street stop-and-searches. Officers themselves filed off each registration number, rendering a gun untraceable.

Perez explained how handy the weapons were to concoct an acceptable story when cops shot unarmed suspects. A typical case was 21-year-old Juan Saldana, shot in the chest and back by Crash officers during a tense street chase. When searched he was unarmed so, before calling an ambulance, officers planted a gun on him (after carefully wiping off their own prints) and adjusted their version of events. In this case the ambulance arrived too late and Saldana died en route to hospital. Following the death, Crash officers celebrated at the Short Stop sports bar, which became a regular ritual after cop-involved shootings (which rose from three in 1995 to twelve in 1996).

A similar routine occurred in the Ovando shooting, a case Perez was reticent to talk about at first (only admitting he was imprisoned on bogus charges). But detectives eventually located Nene, Ovando's friend, missing since his escape from the crime scene. Alex Macias is his real name and his version of events chimed more with Ovando's story than Perez's tale. Macias hadn't seen Ovando since it happened, so investigators knew they hadn't corroborated their stories. When confronted with this news, Perez admitted Ovando was unarmed and handcuffed when hauled into the observation room with Macias. After releasing Macias, Durden shot Ovando first, then Perez fired another three shots into him 'reflexively' (or perhaps to ensure he wouldn't live to be a witness). Then Durden retrieved a gun stashed in his rucksack and planted it on the body as per usual.

CHIEF PARKS

Chief Williams left the job in 1997, allowing his Assistant Chief Bayan Lewis to serve as interim chief. In August, Deputy Chief Bernard C Parks was officially sworn in as the 52nd chief. An African-American, Parks joined the force in 1965 and worked up through the ranks. Mayor Richard Riordan supported his appointment and a package of reforms designed to produce the New LAPD.

Chief Parks soon provoked a rank-and-file backlash by ordering that every complaint registered against a cop must be fully investigated. The Police Protective League (cop union) moaned that the soaring number of complaints was creating too much additional paperwork. Parks explained that the complaint system was supposed to serve citizens, not the LAPD.

So, in September 1999, it fell to Parks to break news of the Perez investigation to the press. A board of inquiry was formed to report on the situation and Parks accepted their criticisms of Rampart Crash methods. Criticism even came from other LAPD officers, like Commander Dan Koenig, who complained to the inquiry that Rampart Crash organised a swoop on a gang funeral, searching cars and arresting mourners. Parks disbanded all the Crash units, replacing them with tightly supervised anti-gang squads.

As proceedings dragged on, the whole Los Angeles County legislature was exposed to criticism. *The New York Times* claimed to have interviewed five LA judges (most insisting on anonymity) who said they oversaw trials where police officers lied substantially.[27] There were also state prosecutors who had refused to pursue cases because of their lack of faith in police testimonies.

The FBI began an investigation, leading to the trial of 77th Street Division officers Edward Ruiz and Jon Paul Taylor, who pleaded guilty to violating the civil rights of a suspect they tried to frame for burglary. Such back-up investigations were essential, because hardball defence attorneys representing cops accused by Perez undermined his testimony by claiming Perez had lied to frame innocent suspects and was now lying to frame innocent cops.

Chief Parks told the *New York Times* in 2000:

> *The Los Angeles Police Department found the misconduct and immediately took action. In three years . . . we have disciplined over 800 officers and terminated 113. We have had 200 officers leave the department while being investigated . . . a number of officers that we have refused to promote because of their prior disciplinary history.*[28]

However, rank and file conservatism continued to hamper reforms. When Parks asked an internal board of captains to reprimand fourteen officers associated with Rampart, the board only sacked three.

LA's courts were kept busy. Some 70 civil rights lawsuits arising from the Rampart scandal cost the city an estimated $125 million.[29]

The Rampart Crash affair exposed further complications that Parks and LAPD must deal with. Black cops, with their own internal factions and codes of conduct, perpetrated some of the worst practices. It's also alleged that some black cops have partisan allegiances with particular street gangs. David Mack (currently incarcerated for robbery) has been named in connection with the gangland conspiracy that murdered rap star Christopher Wallace (better known as Notorious B.I.G. or Biggie Smalls) in 1997. The rapper was implicated in the ongoing feud between two record labels, LA-based Death Row Records and New York's Bad Boy Records. A clear picture of events in this recondite case has yet to be exposed, but it has ominous implications, linking heinous crimes and gang culture to the core of the multi-million-dollar rap music industry. It also involves family relations traceable to the Black Panther hierarchy, and reveals it was common practice for LAPD officers to clock-off as cops before assuming part-time private security jobs, employed by street gangs.

A TOUCH OF EVIL

Typical of Rampart prosecutions, thanks to Perez, were Sgts. Edward Ortiz and Brian Liddy, and Officer Michael Buchanan, for framing gang members Allan Lobos, Cesar Natividad and Raul Munoz in two separate incidents in 1996.[30] When released, many of the framed prisoners told the investigation they were severely beaten in police custody; one alleged that officers thrust him through a third-floor plate-glass window, and another was used as a battering-ram against a brick wall.

Rafael Perez remains enigmatic, casually explaining his excesses as symptomatic of the cultural milieu akin specifically to Rampart Crash, and the LAPD in general; peer group pressure, camaraderie, demands and expectations. Doubtless this takes its toll. But framing, injuring, perhaps killing innocent people – becoming what he was supposed to be fighting – doesn't happen to all cops, even in Los Angeles. And what of loyalty to his fellow cops and friends? He claims he squealed to protect his wife, but told inquisitors he had betrayed her, frequently away from home, spending his ill-gotten gains on sex parties with other women. He used his crippled, caged victim as a bargaining tool. Whose side was he on?

He told investigators there was a sign over the door in Rampart Crash: 'We intimidate those who intimidate others,'[31] and added, 'Whoever chases monsters should see to it that in the process he does not become a monster himself' (perhaps while assuming a dull Manson-esque grin!).

There's a rogue element to Perez, the Latin American in a white man's force, who socialised mainly with Afro-Americans. Identity crisis, sadism, egomania, invulnerability complex ... Perez also exhibits sociopathic tendencies. He is certainly a very, very bad cop!

ER

Millennium Hallowe'en ... Watch out, the LAPD are about! Following up a noise complaint at a private LA party, cops shot and killed actor Anthony Dwain Lee (renowned for playing the black casualty surgeon in the first two series of TV's hospital drama ER). Officers claimed he was brandishing a gun (which transpired to be a toy) when they entered the building. The inquest concluded this was inconsistent with the victim's wounds, three bullets in the back and one in the back of the head.[32]

It seems almost half of LAPD officers are unable to control their habit of beating up defenceless people, even after work. An anonymous questionnaire completed by a cross-section of LA cops in 2000 revealed that 40 per cent are wife-beaters. Lawyer Bob Mullally assessed the results and found up to 277 potential domestic violence-related crimes were committed. His report details 61 assaults – 28 involving a deadly weapon – six rapes and sodomy.[33]

ACTION REPLAY: LAPD 2002

Seems some boys just can't say 'No',[34] especially if they belong to the Los Angeles Police Department, or the LA borough of Inglewood. In July 2002, at a petrol station in Inglewood, sixteen-year-old Donovan Jackson is arrested and handcuffed for a motoring offence. Officer Jeremy Morse shoves the helpless black student over a car, punches and throttles him as accompanying cops stand by.

Recalling the watershed Rodney King beating, an amateur cameraman filmed the event from his hotel room. Officer Morse was immediately suspended, as the video footage was beamed around the world . . .

BIBLIOGRAPHY

Books, Periodicals, Journals

Lou Canon, 'One Bad Cop', in *The New York Times Magazine*, 1/10/2000.

Richard G Carter, 'Rodney King: No Isolated Case', in Various, *Gauntlet: Exploring The Limits Of Free Expression* (#4, Media Manipulation: issue 2), Port Townsend: Loompanics, 1992.

Mike Davis, *City of Quartz*, London: Pimlico, 1998.

George Jackson, *Soledad Brother: Prison Letters*, Harmondsworth: Jonathon Cape and Penguin Books, 1971.

Captain Arthur W Sjoquist, *Los Angeles Police Department 1869–1984*, Los Angeles: Los Angeles Police Revolver and Athletic Club Inc., 1984.

Websites

American Civil Liberties Union: www.aclu.org
www.channel4.com
www.cnn.com

Justice Department Civil Rights Division:
www.usdoj.gov

Los Angeles County District Attorney: www.da.co.la.us

Los Angeles Police Department: www.lapdonline.org

NOTES
  1. All quotations and statistics in 'Lynch-mob Justice' from Captain Arthur W Sjoquist, *Los Angeles Police*

Department 1869–1984, Los Angeles: Los Angeles Police Revolver and Athletic Club Inc., 1984.

2. All quotations and statistics in 'Red Alert' from Captain Arthur W Sjoquist, *Los Angeles Police Department 1869–1984*, Los Angeles: Los Angeles Police Revolver and Athletic Club Inc., 1984.

3. All quotations and statistics in 'Rotten to the Core' from Captain Arthur W Sjoquist, *Los Angeles Police Department 1869–1984*, Los Angeles: Los Angeles Police Revolver and Athletic Club Inc., 1984.

4. All quotations and statistics in 'Gun Law' from Captain Arthur W Sjoquist, *Los Angeles Police Department 1869–1984*, Los Angeles: Los Angeles Police Revolver and Athletic Club Inc., 1984.

5. Mike Davis, *City of Quartz*, London: Pimlico, 1998, p. 271.

6. Ibid., p. 294.

7. Ibid., p. 294.

8. Ibid., p. 294.

9. Ibid., p. 295.

10. Ibid., p. 295.

11. George Jackson, *Soledad Brother: Prison Letters*, Harmondsworth: Jonathon Cape and Penguin Books, 1971, p. 36.

12. To be elected a Republican Senator.

13. Mike Davis, *City of Quartz*, London: Pimlico, 1998, pp. 271–2.

14. Ibid., p. 272.

15. Los Angeles Police Department website.

16. Mike Davis, *City of Quartz*, London: Pimlico, 1998, p. 273.

17. *Herald Examiner*, 14/1/90.

18. Mike Davis, *City of Quartz*, op. cit., p. 275.

19. Ibid., p. 276.

20. *The Times*, 22/12/88.

21. Statistics: Los Angeles Police Department website (for 1991/2).
22. In Richard G Carter, 'Rodney King: No Isolated Incident' in *Gauntlet: Exploring the Limits of Free Expression*, p. 59.
23. All quotations: Lou Canon, 'One Bad Cop', in *The New York Times Magazine*, 1/10/2000.
24. Lou Cannon, *The New York Times Magazine*.
25. All quotations: Lou Canon, op. cit.
26. Ibid.
27. Ibid.
28. Ibid.
29. Website: CNN.com.
30. 2001 Cable News Network.
31. Lou Canon, 'One Bad Cop', op. cit.
32. Report on: About.com (website).
33. Report on: www.feminist.org/news/newsbyte.
34. Incidentally, in January and February 2002, there were 63 gang killings in LA (three times up on the same months in 2000; source: *Guardian Unlimited*, 2002).

4. FEAR AND LOATHING IN CALIFORNIA

OAKLAND RIDERS: THE FUTURE OF LAW ENFORCEMENT?
Chris Barber

The streets of San Francisco and the Bay area enter the twenty-first century patrolled by a mysterious new regime of cop-squad. Known as the 'Oakland Riders', they give away cocaine to innocent passers-by, enforce ritualistic foot-fetishism and shoot pet dogs on sight! Sounds like a future-shock dystopia from a science-fiction novel. Are these Keystone antics the result of drug-crazed Haight Ashbury rejects infiltrating the police force or are more sinister forces running amok? A new recruit blows the whistle, exposing today's all-too-real Oakland Riders . . .

Keith Batt is a fresh-faced, idealistic new police recruit, barely out of his teens when he graduates from Oakland's 146th Cadet Academy, raring to hit the streets, protect law-abiding citizens and fight the good fight against crime. It's June 2000 and in the tradition of countless rookie predecessors, Officer Batt is assigned to work the nightshift (9 p.m. to 7 a.m.), or 'graveyard beat' as old hands call it, in rough inner-city West Oakland. He is teamed up under the supervision of a training officer, 35-year-old Clarence 'Chuck' Mabanag, a wise-assed veteran.

Oakland is a poor, overcrowded neighbourhood, predominately populated by blacks, Hispanics, and howling packs of stray hounds left to rot by the WASP community. It boasts the highest crime figures in northern California, which are largely drug-related. Local street gangs call the turf 'Ghost Town', because of its endless streets of eerie derelict Victorian houses and frequent rattle of surrounding gunfire.

INITIATION RITES

This is a macho work environment and his hard-boiled peer group eyes the young-buck cop with suspicion; he has to act tough and grow up fast, grab any opportunity to prove himself to compatriots. As well as Mabanag, another three or four cops share the beat, officers Frank Vazquez (aged 44), Jude Siapno (32) and Matthew Hornung (29); Officer Bruce Vallimont's name also crops up.

On Batt's first shift (19 June 2000), Mabanag drives him over to meet the guys. Immediately pulling rank, he lectures the novice on house rules and appropriate behaviour. 'You better not be a snitch . . .' Mabanag warns him. 'What goes on in the car, stays in the car.'[1]

Batt notices how close-knit the four officers are, forming their own little street gang, aloof from their surroundings, with clandestine nods and winks, indifferent to external authority. Mabanag continues to instruct Batt on required protocol: 'Fuck all that you learned in the academy. Fuck probable cause. Just jump out and grab the motherfuckers. If you're a coward I'll terminate you myself. If you're a snitch I'll beat you myself . . . Snitches lie in ditches.'

'Are you ready to see the dark side?' Siapno interrupts, bracing Batt for the night ahead . . .

First emergency call received between 1 and 2 a.m., a stolen car report from Mr Kenneth Soriano, block 2500, Adeline Street. Soriano greets the officers on his doorstep, describing his cousin's vehicle and inviting them inside. But Mabanag notices a dog roaming around and threatens to shoot the pet if it comes within range. This winds-up their host, who admonishes the officer.

Mabanag takes umbrage at Soriano's disrespect and loses his rag, smashing Soriano's skull on the sidewalk and choking the hapless victim. Soriano is belligerently handcuffed as blood pours from his head. Siapno and Vazquez appear on the scene, responding to Mabanag's call for back-up and the cop trio put the boot in, mercilessly pounding the surprised, blood-spattered victim.

Having been shown who's in charge, Soriano is ordered to write a statement, as dictated by Mabanag: 'I am sorry for giving the police a hard time. I apologise to the officers and they were not the ones who beat me.'

At the end of the shift, Mabanag is pissed off with Batt, who failed the cop-club's initiation ritual by not laying into the local citizen. But Batt learned his first lesson, that cocky crime victims get bashed into submission!

NEXT WEEK'S THRILLING EPISODE . . .
A week later the shift is too quiet and uneventful for the gang, as Batt and Vazquez patrol the streets in an unmarked OPD van. Shortly after 1.30 a.m. on 32nd Street, Vazquez feels bored when they pass Mr Delhine Allen, strolling home. Vazquez signals Batt to follow and they leap from the van, hurling Mr Allen across the pavement.

Moments later . . . Allen finds himself being shoved into a police car while Mabanag, Hornung and Siapno 'miraculously' arrive at the scene to help out. With meticulous co-ordination, one officer blasts the victim's face with a pepper spray as another repeatedly clubs his feet with a steel truncheon; the other cops jostle to get within range for a few calibrated kicks. 'We're going to find something to put on you,' Mabanag snarls at Allen, as Vazquez produces a rock of crack cocaine.

Siapno improves his creative writing skills, scribbling an official crime report in the car before driving Allen, moaning and bleeding, to an empty car park, hidden under a bridge; time for Siapno to relieve his pent-up frustration with a few hefty whacks and punches to the handcuffed prisoner. 'Ah . . . that's much better!'

By the time the boys in blue have finished, Mr Allen is a mess. His eye is half hanging out, he's swollen and bleeding, and unable to walk. The officers reluctantly decide to ferry him to the nearest casualty ward. But at least they haven't lost their sense of humour as Vazquez chuckles, 'They're gonna have to peel that guy's cornea off Jude's elbow.'

Tired after another night of jolly japes, the gang book Mr Allen into jail and clock off. Mabanag is annoyed and eyes Batt suspiciously, because the tyro hadn't enthusiastically joined in the beating. In future, Batt was ordered, he must keep battering the prisoner until told to stop.

According to Officer Siapno's report, Delhine Allen was seen discarding rocks of crack cocaine.

Officer Keith Batt continues to learn the ropes and tries to do his job for over a week. But he's a bit of a wimp and the stress of watching surprised citizens get beaten black 'n' blue night after night, and having trumped-up charges pinned on them by uniformed law officers, takes its toll. He's clearly the sensitive type and hands in his resignation – after reporting everything he witnessed to Oakland Police Department Internal Affairs section.

THE CASE IN HAND
Batt alleges his fellow officers assaulted, beat up, and planted evidence or filed fictitious charges on at least ten

people; all, *coincidentally*, happen to be Afro-Americans. The last incident he witnessed concerned cops planting seventeen rocks of crack on nineteen-year-old Rodney Mack, after busting a dice game on 3 July 2000.

Mack was imprisoned for over a month before the charges were dropped. His solicitor Jim Chanin told the *Holland Sentinel*:

> *They could've arrested him for playing dice. There was pressure to clean up the area and what better way to show that than with a large number of drug arrests . . . Many of these officers are young people in their twenties and when they hear the mayor of a city making warlike statements, that this drug activity should be stopped at any cost, those directives can be misapplied. That may be what happened here.*
> *(November 2000)*

Chanin was the first lawyer (in this case) to launch proceedings against the city police department for abuse of civil rights. He immediately focuses attention on Oakland's local politics and interference in law enforcement by elected officials.

A couple of years prior, Oakland's Mayor Jerry Brown won election on a robust law and order ticket. In addition to the usual 'clean up the streets 'n' lock up the creeps' rhetoric, Brown offered a cash incentive. All the surrounding neighbourhoods had recently received huge cash investment for civic development and regeneration, by attracting businesses to relocate to them. Already being the poorest and shabbiest locale in the region, West Oakland missed the boat. But Brown promised voters the constituency was next in line for speculators, if voters elected him to get tough on crime.

After winning, Brown promptly sacked Oakland's popular police chief, replacing him with Chief Richard Word and a vigilant crusade against crime. This involved encouraging cop boot-boy tactics, with Brownie points awarded to officers busting drug-related street crime. From 1998 to 1999, crime figures dropped by 15.8 per cent – twice the national average among a population of 370,000. It's not really surprising if residents were reluctant to call the cops or report crimes, due to mounting fear of redneck police tactics. But cut-throat partisan politics ushered in statistical policing and, for cops on the beat, the pressure was on to increase the drug-bust rate by any means necessary.

SILENCE IN COURT

In November 2000, following an internal inquiry by the Police Department into Batt's allegations, Vazquez, Mabanag, Siapno and Hornung were fired and charged with offences including assault, kidnapping and filing false reports. Shortly thereafter, Vazquez disappeared and remains at large, thought to be lying low in Mexico with the FBI in hot pursuit and a $200,000 warrant on his head. The other three Riders hired high-profile defence attorneys, who prepared for battle against counsel for the prosecution, Alameda County District Attorney Tom Orloff's office, in a protracted cut 'n' thrust court case.

Aged 23 when preliminaries began, Keith Batt was rewarded for his scruples with another job in the police force. However, he was moved to the appropriately named Pleasanton Police Department, a quieter, more comfortable neighbourhood. Less fortuitous (he admitted), his first task was to serve as chief prosecution witness on the ensuing case.

While manning nine 'graveyard' shifts, Batt witnessed the Riders instigate unprovoked attacks on eleven citizens, and jail seven people on trumped-up drugs-related charges. A watertight prosecution case was built around eight specific incidents, which Batt would recount to the court. Although he told the prosecution about more illegal Rider activities, it was considered strategically advantageous to limit their arguments to a few clear-cut events, involving a lot of serious charges. (This is common practice in North American and European law courts, to avoid confusing the jury and limit the counter tactical manoeuvres available to the defence.) However, in a sensitive case like this, partisan groups can protest that the state apparatus is conspiring to minimise damage to its institutions by failing to expose the full magnitude of the crimes (perhaps with some justification?). In this instance, the eight incidents enabled the prosecution to charge Mabanag, Hornung and Siapno with 26 criminal counts.

Controversial from the outset, it took over a year for the trial proper to begin, before Alameda County Superior Court Judge Leo Dorado. Kim Curtis reported:

> *Three former Oakland police officers systematically set up young black men and conjured false accusations against them to feed their egos . . .*
>
> *'The defendants, their squad, worked virtually unsupervised,' Alameda County Deputy District Attorney David Hollister said . . . during his opening statement. 'They found it easy to go off and freelance, to work on their own, to gather in force to jump out of their vehicle and grab somebody.' . . . Went too far in their quest to increase their arrest numbers.*
>
> *'The defendants fed off this attention,' Hollister said. 'They liked being looked up to by the younger officers.'*

> *... Defence lawyers ... say the officers simply were doing their jobs in a tough neighbourhood. All have pleaded innocent.*
>
> *Mike Rains, Mabanag's lawyer, said the officers are scapegoats. The scandal resulted in the dismissal of about 90 criminal cases.*[2]

As the case gathered momentum, Batt gave evidence from the stand for over a week.

According to Riders' folklore, their name was based on a report by an unnamed day-shift cop, who had routinely stopped and questioned a citizen before politely sending him on his way. The person got agitated when stopped, but was so relieved by the officer's friendly demeanour that he thanked him, and then warned the cop to watch out for 'The Riders', who patrolled the streets after midnight, beating up citizens and putting 'dope on them'.

Batt told the court how Mabanag loved this tale:

> *He retold the story several times nightly and thought it was funny. It wasn't formally defined who was a Rider and who was not, but I had an understanding who wanted to be involved ... It was clear who stayed together and who kept their distance.*

Oakland Riders is also the name of the local softball team, a connection they relished. During Batt's first week, an officer from the precinct broke his leg. A softball was passed around the locker room to be signed by initiates as a get-well gift. It was styled to resemble the autographed balls handed out by team members to their fans. When the ball was handed to Batt, Siapno intervened to stop him signing it, announcing Batt was not yet a Rider.

The prosecution, as evidence in the Riders trial, later produced the ball. 'Riders' had been lovingly inscribed on it in large letters and the monikers were authentically inked. Batt was asked to read out the names when giving evidence: ' "Chuck X" Mabanag, "St. Jude" Siapno, "Space Monkey" Hornung, and Vazquez.'

Siapno frequently had his leg pulled for his foot fetish, because he won notoriety from workmates at the precinct for hitting people's feet with his baton. This eccentricity earned him another nickname: the 'foot doctor'.

Vazquez was nicknamed 'choker', and he is short with close-cropped hair, a pockmarked face, an earring in one ear, and bears a tattoo on his right arm displaying his wife's name, Pilar. Batt said:

Among other officers who worked West Oakland, the Riders were admired and feared . . . If you weren't in that group, you stayed away.[3]

Testifying about his instruction in Riders' methods, Batt explained the 'trick' of writing fraudulent crime reports, to justify their tactics:

I was realising that my field training was falsifying a police report. It bothered me . . . I knew it wasn't the right thing to be doing.

Nevertheless, he did as he was told – even copying false reports verbatim, believing Mabanag could get him fired if he refused. Further, Batt said he was afraid high-ranking officers at the precinct might unofficially con-done Rider tactics; certainly the clique's bust-record had earned them respect from superiors. Wearing his new cop uniform in the stand, while staring across at the defendants (his former workmates), Batt alleged the Riders regularly toured drug-dealing hotspots in an unmarked van, randomly choosing passers-by to assault and plant drugs on. Back at the station, Sergeant Jerry Hayter, the nightshift supervisor, repeatedly ignored prisoners' claims of being set up and beaten up.

Prompted by Hollister, counsel for the state prosecution service, Officer Batt recalls details from each of his shifts. From his first night on the job, he describes the encounter with Soriano, how Mabanag had intended to cause a fight to inculcate Batt in the action. In this way, Batt would have been initiated into the Riders via active participation in committing a crime. One for all and all for one, Batt could not have betrayed the 'team' without risking his own complicity and being exposed by a partner in crime; corroborated by the victim if in dispute. But that's not how it turned out, hence Mabanag's increasing frustration each night, as Batt shied away from the violence.

The cross-examination Batt endured, from hardball defenders, was gruelling and relentless. He is accused of lacking the 'metal' to fight crime on Oakland's tough streets. Defence lawyer Mike Rains stated: 'Keith Batt is cunning, deceitful and cannot be trusted.'

VICTIMS

After Batt, the prosecution calls its other witnesses, mainly former victims of the Riders. Many were pardoned for wrongful conviction (having been busted by the Riders) and released from incarceration. Some have unrelated criminal records, allowing the defence to challenge their evidence; others had clean records before encountering the Riders. At least 116 Oakland residents are suing the city and Police Department over civil rights abuses perpetrated by the Riders. All are Afro-Americans and remuneration will run into millions of dollars, possibly busting the city's budget.

One of the first Rider victims to testify against the cops was dog owner Kenneth Soriano, aged 20, who mostly corroborated Batt's version of events, explaining how, during the struggle, Mabanag 'grabbed me in a choke hold, in like a sleeper hold'. Soriano pointed to the scar over his eye, from the beating he sustained; despite falsifying his statement, the Riders never bothered to charge him with any crime (that he hadn't committed!).

Typically, another victim was Anthony Miller, aged 43, falsely accused of possessing cocaine after police on Market Street stopped him on 20 June 2000.

And another (pre-dating Batt's tour of duty): Gregory Nash was crossing the road at Telegraph in February 2000 when a van recklessly raced past, narrowly missing the pedestrian. Nash furiously gesticulated rude signals at the vehicle, which suddenly screeched to a halt. Five plain-clothed Riders leapt out, including Vasquez, who grabbed Nash by the neck, shouting 'Fucking Nigger!' Officers bundled Nash into the van and obtained his address – a health farm where he also worked as a live-in security guard. The cops had a field day, reducing Nash's company pad to a demolition site. Vasquez waved a bag in front of Nash containing crack and a crack pipe, saying, 'This is yours.' On top of his pending court case for narcotics possession, Nash was sacked and evicted by his employer over the affair.

COP-SHOT DOG-WATCH
Nightshift was 'graveyard beat' to veteran cops, but 'dogwatch' in Riders' rap. Perhaps because pet dogs – and their female owners – were not exempt from the Riders' peculiar notion of justice and intimidation, as testified by Janice Stevenson. Janice was at home on

Chestnut Street in June 2000, when a truckload of cops arrived on her doorstep with a search warrant for the premises. Among them were officers Siapno, Mabanag and Vazquez. The pad was thought to be a drug den (officers claimed). Siapno ventured into the backyard to continue the search but was confronted by Janice's pit bull terrier, chained to a big garden post. So he shot it in the head and felt much better. Jane was most upset when she arrived in the garden, while Siapno claimed he was very sorry, but the mutt had leapt at him in a surprise attack. Now the dog's skull was splattered over the dung heap as its headless corpse spurted blood on the lawn. Although too distraught to argue, Janice clearly remembered chaining dog to pole; what's more, she had warned Siapno about the dog before he went in the garden. No drugs were discovered and, as the cops marched out, Janice noticed the Riders whispering to each other and chuckling about the dead dog.

No further action was taken, but Janice was surprised when shown her statement (from the dog-day) in court. She remembered completing only half the page and signing the bottom, but now the empty lines were filled with a description of her dog, wildly charging around the neighbourhood, snapping at passing schoolkids.

The first lawsuit settlement awarded to a Riders' victim was for $195,000, in February 2002, paid by the city council to compensate the plaintiff, Mr Kenneth Davis. Davis served 287 days in custody before his disputed arrest conviction was quashed by the Supreme Court, ordering his immediate release.

CLIFFHANGER: THE CASE CONTINUES . . .
OK, you have the gist of it now. It's the same old story, so let's leave the courtroom drama as a cliffhanger, with years to run and millions of dollars being frittered away

on overpaid legal teams making endless objections to reality while citing increasingly ludicrous points of arcane statutes. Meanwhile, vote-grabbing politicians out-bluff each other on get-tough law enforcement . . . banner-waving protestors shriek civil rights . . . and even more lawyers sue everyone for even more cash. There's a dangerous psycho-cop on the loose, crossing borders incognito with the FBI's finest in hot pursuit. Sure to run and run in seat-gripping news flashes, disrupting the commercial breaks.

Police Chief Word told the media that all Riders had been completely eradicated from the 'Oakie' force by mid-summer 2000. He insisted the four cops charged represented the only bad cops in his force and all would be convicted. In 2001, Jamil Muwwakkil was clubbed and beaten to death by six Oakland police officers.[4] Clearly they are not bad cops, because no one was sacked, prosecuted or reprimanded. Nor has the Department officially apologised since the killing.

Perhaps they're just typical Oakie cops?

PARALLEL LINES

There are similarities with LA's Rampart Crash saga (Perez *et al.*), which have been exhaustively explored by American commentators. For the benefit of those of you with better things to do than stuff your anoraks with trivia on colloquial Americana throughout the last century, there was an established tradition of inter-city rivalry between California's two Pacific, metropolitan cultural centres. Hence the overzealous enthusiasm of hacks to overadumbrate the all too obvious parallels – while failing to notice subtler contrasts (the latter potentiating deeper insights into each case).

Both scandals were exposed within close proximity; the Riders inquiry augmented while legal proceedings, lawsuits and media attention continued occurring in the Rampart case (2000).

However, in the Riders saga, both the internal police inquiry and subsequent prosecution case have (at least in public) chosen to limit their scope to the minimum number of personnel implicated in the conspiracy, and within the shortest acceptable time frame. Defence counsel for the Riders contends the cops on trial are scapegoats. It has been publicly admitted that Oakland Police Chief Word agreed the Department would co-operate with prosecutors, only providing the case was limited to the four officers charged and the investigation into past conduct would go back only a short period prior to Batt joining the force.

Civil rights groups and the media have highlighted the inadequacy of these limitations. It's surely unlikely that this extent of criminal policing (achieved by the Riders) and their apparent confidence could have developed in total isolation from the rest of the precinct. Further, the investigation into LA's Rampart conspiracy had far more resources at its disposal and more co-operation from the Police Chief. This enabled the internal inquiry and prosecutors to complete a more satisfactory investigation (than would have been possible if limited to Perez's testimony).

The Riders conspiracy, like the Rampart conspiracy, appears to have been nurtured in comparable working conditions. Conspirators are front-line duty 'troops', serving directly in the firing line of deprived and overcrowded inner-city neighbourhoods, where violence is rampant and crime levels are out of control. Affluent, wealthy districts surround these. Prevailing conditions have developed over many decades of neglect and underinvestment, while local opportunity has been depleted. Both communities inhabit exclusion zones for the people most alienated and ill equipped to deal with mainstream society. Many come from other countries and simply don't know the social responsibilities expected of them, or even understand the language (this point is more apparent in the Rampart case). Lack of jobs and well-organised drug dealing exacerbates problems.

Police officers 'dumped' into these areas are mainly young, raw recruits, lacking the experience, supervision and special training required to cope with these conditions. Unable to gain the trust and support of the communities they 'serve', they are forced to rely totally on their immediate peer group, fellow officers, sometimes while undertaking unpopular, stressful or dangerous tasks. This reliance is unhealthy, stigmatising the officers concerned; leaving them stranded with expectations and responsibilities they cannot possibly meet.

HEART OF DARKNESS

How can you protect and serve the community where there is no functioning community? Amidst a relentless struggle for survival, what peace exists to protect? When law and order offers no benefits, why should punishment deter crime? These are real, hardcore issues, which neither case dared to confront.

Thrown in at the deep end, with only a few officers in the same predicament to share understanding, support and empathy, the nature of the beast changes. In *Critique of Dialectical Reason*, Jean Paul Sartre proposes a model that shows how previously unrelated individuals may happen upon each other, via shared propinquity. Defined through actions in the world, one's relation to others changes, becoming clearer as those performing unrelated actions disappear. The diminishing number of people remaining relate to one another through *seriality*

– forming a series, because each has undertaken similar responsibilities (a queue of people at a bus stop for instance, or police recruits). Separated from 'others' by their shared responsibility (awaiting a particular bus, patrolling beat #99), this series is transformed into a group, defined by their actions. Those continuing grow to recognise each other, *fusing* together in pursuit of 'their' common goal. But the *fused group* who realise this desired end can now only turn to each other for mutual appreciation of their achievement. The fused group becomes institutionalised, each needing the understanding and recognition that can only come from fellow travellers. Unable to move on, or apart, the *institution* is defined by *inertia*. Those outside the institution, the changing exteriority, must be regarded as a threat (incapable of appreciating and perpetuating the self-justifying institution).[5]

The internal dynamics of each 'gang of conspirators' shares self-perpetuating exclusivity. Both groups consist entirely of men, and their ability to survive in hostile terrain depends upon the recognition and support of fellow initiates. For this dependency they need a system of shared values, and they must constantly prove their total loyalty to each other. An idolisation of machismo, of all things masculine reflects an *a priori* commonality. The clearest expression of loyalty between initiates is exhibited in their acts of transgression of wider social taboos, their law breaking either in joint actions or witnessed by each other. This is crucial within a partnership of cops, because (as each is all too aware) it runs completely counter to every value they are expected to uphold as members of the broader 'police gang'. (Hence Perez and co. engage in bank robbery, drug dealing, murder; the Riders humiliate and beat innocent people – particularly those requesting their help as police officers – and also fraudulently complete official police reports.)

ONLY HAVING A LAUGH

Shared jokes, the Riders' exclusive sense of humour (laughing at 'in-group' jokes that outsiders cannot appreciate), suggests a dual function. Socially it strengthens bonding via an exclusive code of communication. Psychologically their laughter at the degradation they're inflicting on others distances them from the horror they're inflicting and helps them reduce their victims to inhuman objects. Such humour was common among Nazi concentration camp guards and it is likely that the Rampart gang also had a good old laugh together.

The episode concerning the origin of the Riders' adopted name, and its popular repetition among initiates, suggests they want to propagate their own group mythology. This is further developed by their adoption of nicknames, which are used between them, thus enhancing intimacy while distancing themselves from their birth names (which connote their exterior roles and family attachments).

Identifying with the Oakland Riders sports team represents another valorisation of male bonding, the gladiatorial all-American, all-male team working together as a unit, competing against others to win. The hometown champions as local heroes.

Racism, as exhibited by the Riders, becomes another tool by which they define their gang as exclusively white and distance themselves as superior, allowing objectification of their victims. The Rampart gang are of mixed race, so their racism is less crude but still apparent; probably a sliding hierarchy of 'non-white' allegiances, based on origin, territory and/or kinship.

PRESTIGE OR PROFIT?

What motivates a cop to rot?

When motives are explored, the Rampart cops are driven by pure greed: cash, dollars, profit. They use their police insider credentials to set up and hold up banks. Suspects (while in their custody) are routinely humiliated, tortured, maimed and murdered, so the cops can steal their cash or confiscate and sell their drugs. Their ill-gotten gains are squandered on high-profile and ostentatious lifestyles. Thrill-crazy and living for kicks, they gamble in casinos, buy hookers for sex parties and live beyond their means. Greed is insatiable and as they grow overconfident, taking more risks, it's greed that is their downfall (stealing cocaine from the precinct stash to sell). Ringleader Perez also has a deeper, darker side; but greed remains the manifest motive.

In contrast, the Riders are motivated by kudos and prestige – ironically in their role as outstanding police officers. Apparently they did not profit from their crimes with material gains. While doing their dull and gruelling jobs they craved recognition and discovered the simplest means to gain status in the force. By randomly arresting and charging innocent citizens they quickly notched up their arrest rate, gaining respect from superior officers and being looked up to by colleagues and fledgling cops. Suddenly and with alacrity they were heroes, achievers and winners, setting the standards to which others aspired.

BLOOD SPORTS AND SEXUAL INTRIGUE

Vazquez, Siapno, Hornung and Mabanag had served in the police force for periods ranging from two to ten years. Vazquez, the fugitive, was the oldest, with a decade on Mabanag (the second oldest) and twenty years on Batt (the baby). An internal order of rank based on respect for age and experience evolved among the Riders, giving Vazquez superiority. But in the wider force, he had not been promoted to a position appropriate to his years of service. While Mabanag served loyally as second in charge to Vazquez, fledgling Batt was expected to obsequiously fall in line under his elders.

What was really going on between this bonded male group, who desperately craved the respect of their superiors and fellow officers while instituting their own exclusive unit? An elite, defined by actively breaking the rules which every cop is supposed to uphold. And, like the Rampart pact, cementing their brotherhood in sadistic, joint bloodletting rituals, wilfully perpetrated on the bodies of helpless victims like sacrificial offerings.

Their sordid working methods, deliberately degrading, humiliating and harming the very weakest citizens whom they were supposed to serve and respect, sometimes in response to those people's calls for help. Misanthropic boot-boys, whom promotion passed by, stuck in a hell-hole with society's wretched outcasts, they were unable to comprehend the scale of crime-ridden deprivation around them, never mind confronting the hopelessness of their inability to improve this environment.

Instead they turned to easy, quick-fix solutions to escape their own misery. Riders confirmed each other's delusions of grandeur. They were superior to the filth and scumbags they policed; upstanding, loyal Americans who deserved better! No, they weren't going to obsequiously run around at the beck and call of inferiors; the Riders would show who was in charge, take control; these riff-raff would be made to cower, suffer and fear their superiors! Beaten into submission, they could be used as objects, bust-statistics, serving their masters' pursuit of rightful respect from the force they had loyally served.

These were the social forces, but there were also the psychological forces at play. In his early work, from *The Function of the Orgasm* to *The Mass Psychology of Fascism*, Wilhelm Reich acknowledges and synthesises both.[6]

Reich was an early pupil of Sigmund Freud, impressed by Freud's analysis of sexual repression. But when Freud concluded this hypothesis was inadequate,[7] Reich tried to demonstrate that sexual potency was a biological instinctive drive.[8] Living in Weimar, Germany, his critical analysis of fascism earned him a place on Hitler's hit-list and he was forced to flee Germany when the Nazis came to power.

At a time when capitalist democracies were most authoritarian and patriarchal, Reich saw sexual liberation as a revolutionary potential, capable of freeing mankind from conformity to authoritarianism. The healthy, liberated citizen is one able to realise ecstatic sexual potential. But the capitalist work ethic depends on repressing people's sex drives in favour of hard work. Capitalism exerts this control through the authoritarian, patriarchal family. Forced to conform to 'moral' authority, sexual potency turns in upon itself, becoming repressed in the psyche. It is held in check with character armour (distorted and unhealthy mental and physical development) and manifests physical symptoms through muscular spasms and aches, as well as latent masochistic tendencies (creating neurosis or psychosis).

In fascists, subservience to authority is most pronounced in latent, repressed homosexuality. Power and liberated desire is surrendered. Excessive masculinity and misogyny manifests through hysterical conformity. Sexual potency and frustrated desire builds internally, until it is forced to erupt (like a volcano) as physical violence, directed against non-conformists who are de-humanised as inferior 'things' (by the repressed fascist).

This model offers a pertinent perspective on the Riders conspiracy and insight into Rampart: idolised masculinity, excessive respect for institutional authority, repressed homosexual desire, de-humanisation of 'outsiders', pent-up frustration erupting as physical violence.

BAD BOY
Both the Riders and Rampart gangs formed clandestine elites, who institutionalised and operated according to their own laws. In a sense these codes of conduct represented the logical apotheosis of the armed, militaristic and uniformed law-enforcing institutions they had already joined. Each considered their internal alliance was vigilant and invincible to external threat. Yet both were eventually exposed and destroyed – betrayed – by one of their own, privy to internal dynamics. However, apart from sharing the same job and uniform, these two agents of chaos are worlds apart.

Rafael Perez is bad to the core. His involvement in the Rampart conspiracy was central, complicit in almost every foul crime committed by his gang; a compulsive liar, even when snitching to police inquisitors. Got himself off lightly with a grass-up deal and unknown hostage, served just three years (see Chapter 3).

BATT IN AGAINST THE RIDERS
Keith Batt, the lone, young rookie cop, new on the job – and perhaps more enigmatic and unique as a police officer than Perez; thrust headfirst into the Riders pack on his first night, patrolling the scariest beat in town. But it wasn't the local drug-peddling street rappers or

bullets ricocheting out of the darkness that freaked him out. It was the veteran, street-wise cops he'd been assigned to work with and learn from. From night one, despite increasing pressure by the night from his mad-pack of seniors, he held back from the savage bloodthirsty beatings his 'colleagues' dealt out to innocent citizens in distress. He watched hawk-eyed, clocking every detail, witnessing one man suffer a broken collarbone, another almost blinded; but not once during the nine shifts he worked did he lift a finger against anyone. The only crime he participated in (under Mabanag's orders) was falsifying official Police Department forms. After battling with his conscience, when he could take no more, he resigned from the job he had coveted since his childhood; he reported the crimes he witnessed to his superiors, freely admitting his own misdemeanour. And he walked out.

That was the last he wanted to hear about it; no way did he want to stand up in court, face his former colleagues and testify for their prosecution. He had done his bit and wanted out. But he was the only one who could do it. The District Attorney threatened, cajoled and finally begged him to stand up for justice. If he wasn't the chief prosecution witness, there would be no prosecution, there was no case. Without his testimony the Riders would continue to inflict fear and terror on this helpless, dysfunctional community. Batt took the stand, giving detailed testimony of everything he witnessed; he remained on the stand day after day, relentlessly grilled and contradicted by top-notch defence lawyers. They called him a cunning liar, namby-pamby coward, a treacherous snitch. Batt didn't crack! Finally he left it to Deputy DA Hollister to summon another witness – Kenneth Soriano, one of many former victims waiting to testify against the Riders.

Extraordinary, brave, exemplary; or dumb, naive, crazy . . . Is this a Good Cop?

BACK TO THE FUTURE OF LAW ENFORCEMENT

Perhaps most significantly, the officers involved in each instance seem to have conspired together under similar circumstances. Intense political rivalry between elected city officials, focusing public and media attention on law and order issues; prompting promises to get tough on crime, by increasing efficiency rather than higher taxes and public spending or examining environmental causes. This necessitating more partisan interference in managing police departments than is salubrious (in the interests of justice). Shake-ups of top-brass appointments are based on ability to manufacture improving, 'feel-good' statistics at the expense of broader managerial abilities. Pressure is filtered down the ranks to notch-up recordable results, as resources are diverted away from other contributing causal factors.

In recent years this growing trend has produced similar results in other American cities. Do people learn from this? Not at all; expect more US cities to repeat this scenario. Seems some politicians, city officials, and privatised prison and security service providers are making big bucks out of the process. The prison business in particular is growing at such a fast rate and generating so much cash flow that it has become integral to the American economy.[9]

Some of the peculiarities pertaining to this disastrous approach suggest only the United States would tolerate these developments. Be warned, where business interests can increase profits and create jobs, while allowing politicians to offer lower taxes and increased efficiency, the current UK trend is to follow.

The law and order ticket remains a trump card where politicians can grab votes; just by repeating the same old 'get tough on punishment' clichés. We always fall for it, despite knowing it doesn't actually deter crime and is the most expensive long-term policy to pursue.

Striving for real and fair justice, and human rights, are not natural phenomena that just appear when conditions are right. Nor are they floating around outside some Platonic cave, if we can just find the exit. They are relative, changing social constructions that come at a price.

HOMESPUN WISDOM OR FISHWIFE'S TALE?

Finally, your writer asks indulgence for a personal (hopefully relevant) recollection. When it came to political or worldly issues, there was nothing my father and I agreed about. Years after his death and I'm still getting angry when remembering his views; but one of his theories keeps recurring, inspiring careful consideration. Somehow it now seems almost agreeable. He proposed that:

> *Police and criminals are basically people sharing similar characteristics. A certain type, whether developed through nature or nurture, will choose between these two occupations. Nothing else will appeal, but they could equally go either way between crook and cop. Neither should be trusted very far; both represent trouble if they choose your life to interfere in and should be handled with extreme caution . . .*

He twittered on about how it's probably better for most of society to get them in uniform and on-side, at least that may give you some control over them.

Just don't turn your back on either of them!

BIBLIOGRAPHY

Books

Wilhelm Reich, *The Function of the Orgasm*, London: Panther Books, 1968.

Charles Rycroft, *Reich*, Glasgow: Fontana, 1972.

Jean Paul Sartre, *Critique of Dialectical Reason*, London: Verso, 1982.

Other

Glen Chapman, 'Attorneys Spar Over Evidence', *The Oakland Tribune*, 4/6/02.

Kim Curtis, 'Prosecutor shows Oakland cops' pattern of setting up suspects', *The Mercury News*, 4/6/02.

Henry K Lee, 'Hearing in Police Misconduct Case', in *San Francisco Chronicle*, 31/3/01.

Wendy Snyder, 'Police Containment', in *Oakland Uhuru News*, 16/7/02.

AC Thompson, 'How to Blow a Police Corruption Case', in *San Francisco Bay Guardian News*, 22/8/01.

Jim Herron Zamora, 'Cop: I was Taught to Lie', in *San Francisco Chronicle*, 18/9/02.

Associated Press, 'Oakland Rocked by Police Scandal', *The Holland Sentinel*, 30/9/00.

NOTES
1. All direct quotations from trial transcripts, as quoted in AC Thompson, 'How to Blow a Police Corruption Case', in *San Francisco Bay Guardian News*, 22/8/01 (except where otherwise stated).
2. Kim Curtis, 'Prosecutor shows Oakland cops' pattern of setting up suspects', *The Mercury News*, 4/6/02.

3. Jim Herron Zamora, 'Cop: I was Taught to Lie', in *San Francisco Chronicle*: 18/9/02.

4. Sealli Moyenda (PDUM representative), Wendy Snyder, 'Police Containment', in *Oakland Uhuru News*, 16/7/02.

5. This is an extreme simplification of a recondite theorem, but Sartre's systematic *intentions* are problematic and its use here is strictly as an analogy.

6. As with Sartre's model cited earlier, it would be foolish to suggest Reich's explanation offers truth or a final solution around which the case could be closed; but where there is actually no final solution, Reich might serve as another analogy or model to focus on.

7. Replacing it with his theory of life and death drives.

8. Further, Reich was the first theorist to attempt to integrate Freudian and Marxist doctrine into a coherent theory of sexual revolution.

9. Pillaging of state responsibilities by greedy, obese businessmen is the other end of the equation; directly reflected in Bad Cop behaviour – from Perez and co. to the Riders Inc.

5. THE BLUE WALL OF SILENCE

THE ASSAULT ON ABNER LOUIMA
Russell Gould

Fidelis Ad Mortem (Faithful Unto Death).
> Motto of the New York Police Department.

I sodomised Mr Louima with a stick, then threatened to kill him if he told anybody . . . I was mad at the time.
> Officer Justin A Volpe admits his guilt
> to the Federal Court

The greatest act of betrayal of one police officer by another is to commit a serious act of misconduct in their presence and put them in the position of having to choose between a false loyalty that risks their livelihood and perhaps even their liberty and obeying their oath of office and testifying truthfully against an officer where it's required.
> US Federal Attorney Zachary Carter reacts to Volpe
> being found guilty of the assault on Louima

THE NYPD, POLICE BRUTALITY AND THE MAYOR

The sadistic assault by members of the New York Police Department on Abner Louima, a 33-year-old recent legal immigrant to the United States from Haiti, took place during the night of 9/10 August 1997. The attack by on-duty officers in the 70th Precinct station house caused widespread protests from the Haitian and other ethnic communities and further damaged the image of the NYPD as details of the racist insults used against Louima and the brutal injuries he suffered became public knowledge. The police officers accused were tried on a number of charges relating to the attack; two of them are at present serving lengthy sentences.

The attack on Louima had political implications; New York City's mayor has responsibility for the management of the city's Police Department. The next mayoral election between the incumbent Rudolph Giuliani and his Democrat opponent David Dinkins was to take place in November 1997. NYPD officers supported Giuliani and his 'zero tolerance' policy regarding crime in New York; Giuliani had defeated the first black mayor, David Dinkins, in 1993. During the Republican crackdown on crime, complaints by blacks about police misconduct had increased dramatically, with community leaders accusing police of using unnecessary force. In the twelve months preceding the attack on Louima, the city of New York had paid out a total of $22m to settle police brutality cases. In addition, the NYPD was also seen as unrepresentative of local communities; the police force at the time of the assault on Louima was 70 per cent white, while 60 per cent of New York's population was non-white.

'Rudy' Giuliani's reputation survived the Louima case; after his victory in the 1997 election, he was feted as an American national hero after his response to the September 11th 2001 terrorist attacks on New York.

THE ASSAULT ON ABNER LOUIMA

Abner Louima, who lived with his wife Micheline and their two children, worked as a security guard at the Spring Creek water and sewage plant in the Flatlands district of Brooklyn. Late on the evening of 9 August 1997 he left work to go to the Club Rendez-vous, a nightclub frequented by Haitians on Flatbush Avenue, to see a Haitian dance band called The Phantoms that was performing there. The club began to wind down at around 3.30 in the morning of 10 August; while people were leaving, a fight between two women broke out in the street. Abner Louima and some other men tried to separate the women, and then a police car came on the scene. One of the officers picked on Louima and started shoving him; a fight between the two swiftly developed and other policemen joined in, managing to subdue Louima who was handcuffed and dragged into a police vehicle. On the ride back to the 70th Precinct station house, Louima alleged that he was punched and hit by the officers in the car who stopped the vehicle twice in order to carry out these assaults.

Abner Louima's initial account of events was as follows:

Arriving at the station at around 4.50 a.m., Louima was taken to a room where his clothes were removed and the money stolen from his wallet. Louima was then subjected to a torrent of racist verbal abuse. Louima was then taken to a toilet room where several of the officers took part in a savage attack on the still-handcuffed man, punching and hitting him. One of the policemen, later identified as Officer Justin A Volpe, forced a toilet plunger handle into his anus, puncturing his intestine and causing damage to his bladder. When this ordeal was over, the toilet plunger was removed – with Volpe proclaiming to Louima, 'That's your shit, nigger,' and then he thrust the soiled plunger handle into Louima's mouth, breaking several of his teeth. Volpe then called Louima a 'stupid nigger' and told him, 'We're going to teach niggers to respect police officers ... this is Giuliani time, it is not Dinkins time' – the latter comment referring to the candidates for post of Mayor of New York City. The officer threatened that he would murder Louima and his family.

Throughout the attack, Louima's screams of pain rang around the precinct building – but no one on duty there responded, or went to investigate the cause of the disturbance. Louima later said that he thought of his wife and children during the attack and prayed – 'I kept saying, please God, don't let me die . . . I was praying to protect my life because if I died I did not know who would take care of my children.'

After being attacked, Louima was charged with disorderly conduct, obstructing police and resisting arrest. He was then taken to a holding cell, bleeding heavily, and left there.

LOUIMA TAKEN TO HOSPITAL

The desk sergeant on duty that night at the 70th Precinct building, Jeffrey Fallon, claimed to have phoned for an ambulance on seeing Louima escorted into the building. However, no ambulance arrived until 6.25 a.m., and finally left taking Louima to hospital at 7.58 a.m., accompanied by a police escort.

Visiting Abner Louima in the intensive care ward of Coney Island hospital on the Sunday, his relatives were shocked by his injuries, which included a ruptured bladder and a colon so damaged that he had to undergo a colostomy. Making enquiries, they found that none of the officers at the 70th Precinct had reported the incident. They then made contact with the NYPD's Internal Affairs Bureau, notifying them of the injuries they had seen and of Louima's claim that he had been assaulted. An anonymous police officer from the 70th Precinct – later identified as Officer Eric Turetzky – had also reported the incident to the Bureau that day. Investigators tried to speak to Louima in his hospital bed on the morning of Monday 11 August, but he was in no fit condition to speak. They returned the following day and showed him photographs of officers serving in the 70th Precinct; from these pictures, Louima was able to identify two of the policemen involved.

CITY AND POLICE REACTIONS

At a press conference on the afternoon of 13 August, Mayor Giuliani condemned the attack on Louima: 'The alleged conduct involved is reprehensible done by anyone at any time. Done by police officers, it's even more reprehensible.' On the following day, the mayor ordered that the commander of the 70th Precinct, the executive officer and eight other policemen be transferred from active duty. He also commented on the 'Giuliani time' comments allegedly made by Volpe and stated that any police officer who said such a thing 'doesn't deserve to be a member of the New York Police Department'. Giuliani added that NYPD officers should be 'revulsed and repulsed' by what had happened to Louima. Also on 14 August, New York Police Commissioner Howard Safir told the press that he didn't consider the attack on Louima to be an act of police brutality but a 'criminal act committed by people who are criminals'. The NYPD then announced that all charges against Louima had been dropped.

Giuliani visited Louima in hospital – the first of two visits during which the mayor expressed his sorrow and regret at what had happened.

OFFICER VOLPE TURNS HIMSELF IN: OFFICERS ACCUSED

On the evening of 13 August 1997, 70th Precinct Officer Justin Volpe, aged 27, who lived in Staten Island, turned himself in to the NYPD Internal Affairs Bureau in connection with the attack on Louima. He was charged with assaulting Louima.

On 14 August, Police Commissioner Safir, realising that a major incident had taken place that could do untold harm to relations with the local community and do immense damage to the reputation of the NYPD, ordered immediate changes at the 70th Precinct. Desk Sergeant Fallon was suspended and ten other policemen were put on desk duties, pending investigations. These officers included Thomas Bruder and Michael Bellomo. Officer Charles Schwarz was taken off duties and also charged with assaulting Louima.

PROTESTS: 16–17 AUG 1998
Over the weekend of 16–17 August thousands of protesters besieged the 70th Precinct house, many of them waving Haitian flags and some brandishing toilet plungers. Their mood was angry, with chants of 'Sodomites, sodomites' aimed at police.

Black activist and Democratic mayoral candidate Rev. Al Sharpton joined the protestors and addressed the crowd, telling them that the issues in this case were not racial, but were about police brutality. Sharpton met with Louima, and became an unofficial adviser to him and his family.

Also during the weekend, investigators searched the station house and nearby sewers and drains in an attempt to find the toilet plunger used in the assault. They found nothing.

OFFICER WEISE COMES FORWARD
On 17 August, Officer Thomas Weise, who was the working partner of Charles Schwarz, gave investigators his account of events. Weise said that Volpe acted alone in assaulting Louima, and that he and Schwarz had been doing paperwork and looking after a stray puppy during the time that Louima had been at the 70th Precinct building. Weise claimed to have seen Louima and Volpe in the same toilet stall, with the officer brandishing a toilet plunger dripping with excrement; when Weise asked Volpe what had happened, he was told that

Louima had an incontinence problem. This conflicted with Officer Turetzky's earlier claim to have seen Schwarz taking Louima, who at the time had his trousers around his knees, from a cell to a toilet where, Turetzky had told investigators, he had seen Schwarz and Volpe both involved in the assault.

MORE OFFICERS HELD – AND MORE CHARGES

On 18 August two more 70th Precinct officers were charged; Officer Weise – who had offered testimony to investigators the day before – and Officer Thomas Bruder were charged with assaulting Louima in the patrol car after he had been arrested outside the Club Rendez-vous.

That morning, Volpe and Schwarz appeared in the Brooklyn State Supreme Court and pleaded not guilty to charges of sexual abuse and assault. Both men walked from the courtroom, each leaving $100,000 as bail.

It was also revealed that the gloves worn by Justin Volpe during the assault on Louima had been found and were being sent off for analysis. Abner Louima's attorneys announced that they would be suing the city of New York for $55m in damages.

On 21 August, Volpe, Schwarz, Weise and Bruder were indicted on additional charges of second-degree assault on account of the racially biased attitudes they had displayed towards Louima.

CONFLICTING ACCOUNTS

Journalist Garry Pierre-Pierre's interview with Louima in hospital was published in the *New York Times* of 22 August. Louima urged Haitians to attend an anti-police brutality demonstration planned for August 29 and complained of having experienced racist attitudes since moving to America. He did not give details of his arrest and his treatment at the hands of police officers at the 70th Precinct, but did say that during the attack he had feared for his life but was now able to forgive those who had assaulted him.

On the same day the *New York Daily News* published an interview with Volpe in which he claimed 'It wasn't me' that assaulted Louima, and that the injuries had occurred before police had arrived at Flatbush Avenue. Bruder and Weise appeared in court and pleaded their innocence on the second-degree assault charges.

On 26 August the *New York Times* carried an interview with Magalie Laurent, a nurse at the Coney Island Hospital. She claimed that the police who accompanied Louima to the hospital had told doctors that his injuries had been received during homosexual activities. The paperwork police brought with Louima – the Medical Treatment of Prisoners form, also known as PD 244-150 – stated that Louima had suffered 'trauma to rectum' – with no cause given for this injury.

LOUIMA OUT OF HOSPITAL

On 10 October 1997, Abner Louima left hospital under police escort. He was still suffering from the effects of severe internal injuries and was on medication for blood clots in his legs, caused by the beating and having to spend so long immobile in a hospital bed. In addition he was suffering from psychological trauma; his cousin and spokesman for the family Samuel Nicholas told a *New York Times* reporter, 'We don't know how he's going to deal with his life'.

PRE-TRIAL SESSIONS – FEDERAL PROSECUTORS TAKE OVER

In mid-February 1998, defence attorneys and prosecutors met with a judge at the Brooklyn State courthouse to prepare for the trial of the accused police officers. At the same time, Federal prosecutors were considering whether the case should be taken over by them. In the charges in this case, Federal prosecution would carry heavier penalties than a State prosecution.

On 26 February, the Federal prosecutors filed Federal civil rights charges against Volpe, Bruder, Schwarz and Weise. This move superceded the previous State charges. Volpe and Schwarz faced additional Federal charges: Volpe was accused of sexual assault on Louima with the toilet plunger, and Schwarz with holding Louima while Volpe attacked him. Bellomo and Volpe were also charged with civil rights offences for having wrongly arrested and assaulted Patrick Antoine, an eyewitness to the events outside the Club Rendez-vous.

Volpe and Schwarz now faced, if convicted, sentences of life in prison. Additionally, Sergeant Michael Bellomo, who had been the supervisor in charge at the 70th Precinct on the night of the assault on Louima, was charged with lying to investigators.

At the Federal District Court in Brooklyn, presided over by Judge Eugene H Nickerson, all officers pleaded not guilty to all of the charges. In February 1998 it was also announced that Louima's attorneys in the $55m lawsuit against New York City would include Johnnie Cochran and Barry Scheck, who had successfully represented OJ Simpson at his trial at which he was accused of the murder of Nicole Simpson and Ronald Goldman.

FEDERAL GRAND JURY EXPANDS INDICTMENT

Hearings continued and briefs were filed as prosecutors and attorneys set their cases before the judge. On 13 November 1998 the Grand Jury made additional charges of obstruction of justice against Schwarz, Weise and Bruder. They were accused of lying to investigators about what they had witnessed of the attack on Louima in the precinct toilet.

FIRST TRIAL OF POLICE OFFICERS
On 3 May 1999, after five weeks of selection from a preliminary panel of 85, a jury – eight whites, three Hispanics and one black – was finally chosen for the trial of Volpe, Schwarz, Weise, Bruder and Bellomo.

Charges by Federal prosecutors were:
- Volpe, Schwarz, Weise and Bruder – violation of Louima's civil rights during the beating in the police car.
- Volpe – assault on Louima in the 70th Precinct building.
- Schwarz – holding Louima down while Volpe attacked him.
- Bellomo – covering up the beating in the police car.

The trial started on 4 May when Prosecutor Kenneth Thompson opened by listing the complaints against the officers. Thompson alleged that Louima's treatment had been 'cruel' and amounted to 'torture . . . cruel and inhumane'. Volpe's lawyer, Marvyn Kornberg, then told the jury that Louima had lied in order to get a multi-million dollar compensation payment, that Louima's injuries were 'not consistent with a non-consensual insertion of an object into his rectum' and that the 'Giuliani time' accusations were not true. Louima, Kornberg said, had lied 'to create diversiveness in the City of New York'. Atttorneys for the other accused officers declared their clients were innocent of all charges.

On 6 May Abner Louima took the stand. Questioned at first by the prosecutors, he gave details of the assault on him by Volpe who he said had threatened to kill him and his family if he were to make a complaint about what had happened. Declaring in heavily accented English that he had been punched and kicked in the 70th Precinct building by police, and that he was taken to a toilet where 'Officer Volpe put an object in my rectum and pulled it out and he put it in my mouth', Louima also admitted that he had lied when accusing Volpe of having declared 'It's Guiliani time'. Volpe's attorney, Kornberg, then began his cross-examination of Louima, accusing him of lying in order to get money from his civil suit against New York City and the NYPD. He pressed Louima on his 'Giuliani time' accusation; Louima admitted, 'I did it to get the mayor's attention and the attention of people responsible for justice'. Kornberg also raised the issue of the item used in the assault, previously thought to be a toilet plunger. By the time of the trial, prosecutors were claiming that Louima had been attacked with a broomstick – Louima said that just before the assault in the toilet he had seen Volpe pick up an object from the floor, and had assumed it was a toilet plunger. Defence lawyers continued their questioning of Louima, concentrating on Louima's lie re 'Giuliani time' and other inconsistencies in his account of events. Louima said he had perjured himself due to his mind being affected by pain-killing medication that he had been prescribed.

Police officers from the Precinct were then questioned about the attack, breaking the so-called 'blue wall of silence' which reputedly prevents NYPD officers testifying against each other.

On 14 May, Officer Eric Turetzky described having seen Louima, his trousers below his knees, being taken out of the toilet at the precinct by Volpe, who was holding a three-foot-long stick. Turetzky confirmed that

Schwarz had been involved in taking Louima towards the toilet again following the assault by Volpe. Defence lawyers accused Turetzky of making accusations against other officers because he was frightened about what might happen to him if he was implicated in the attack on Louima in the police car as Turetzky had been one of the officers who had been called to the fracas outside the Club Rendez-Vous. On 18 May a second 70th Precinct officer, Mark Schofield, gave evidence against Volpe, claiming that the accused policeman had borrowed gloves from him before the attack on Louima and then returned them covered in blood. Schofield also said he had seen Volpe holding a stick-like object when he had borrowed the gloves.

On 20 May Sergeant Kenneth Wernick told the court of how Justin Volpe had boasted to him of the attack on Louima, claiming that he had inserted the stick five or six inches into Louima's anus and then put it into the victim's mouth. Wernick said that Volpe had shown him the stick and had invited another officer to smell it. A fourth officer, Michael Schoer, testified on the same day that Volpe had waved the stick in his face and invited him to smell it, and that Volpe had told him that the brown stain on the stick was human faeces.

Possibly due to the NYPD's culture of loyalty to their fellow officers and fear of being branded a 'rat', none of these officers had come forward immediately to tell investigators what had happened. In court none of them said they had witnessed the attack on Louima, making their evidence circumstantial.

On 25 May, Justin A Volpe formally changed his plea to guilty on all charges. In tears, he told the court that he had got into a fight with Louima outside Club Rendez-vous and that he had hit Louima in the patrol car on the way to the 70th Precinct building. Then he confessed: 'While in the bathroom of the precinct, in the presence of another officer, I sodomised Mr Louima with a stick, then threatened to kill him if he told anybody . . . I was mad at the time.' Questioned by Judge Nickerson as to his motives for assaulting Louima, the following exchange took place:

> Nickerson: *Going back to the assault in the bathroom and when you put the stick out towards his face, having shoved it into his rectum, was a part of your effort to humiliate him?*
>
> Volpe: *I was in shock at the time, Your Honor. I intended to show it to him because – I couldn't believe what happened. Yes, if that's humiliating him, I'm sure it did.*
>
> Nickerson: *Well, you intended to humiliate him, did you? You thought you were mad at him?*
>
> Volpe: *I was mad at the time, yes.*
>
> Nickerson: *You intended to humiliate him?*
>
> Volpe: *Yes.*

Volpe also told the judge that he would be refusing to testify against his fellow officers, and made an apology for what had happened – not to Louima, but to his own family for the hurt he had caused them.

On 26 May, the trial of the other four officers continued. The prosecution rested its case on 28 May, based largely on Louima's testimony. On 2 June the defence rested its case; none of the four defendants chose to testify. Attorneys for the officers asked for the case against them to be thrown out due to insufficient evidence, but this was refused by Judge Nickerson. Closing arguments were made; the prosecution emphasising the brutality of the attack and how Volpe was not acting alone; the defence attorneys maintaining their clients' innocence while condemning the brutal actions of Justin Volpe.

On 4 June the jury began their deliberations, and delivered their verdict four days later. Schwarz was found guilty of beating Louima outside the toilet and holding him down while Volpe attacked him with the stick. Schwarz, Weise and Bruder were acquitted of charges of assaulting Louima in the patrol car, and Bellomo was acquitted of charges of lying in order to cover up criminal acts by fellow officers.

After the jury announced the verdicts, US Attorney Zachary Carter said that Schwarz, Bruder and Weise would still be tried for conspiracy to obstruct justice. On 22 June 1999 Officers Rolando Aleman and Francisco Rosario were indicted on charges of lying to investigators.

VOLPE SENTENCED

On 13 December 1999, Justin Volpe was given thirty years in prison for his assault on Louima. The maximum sentence for the crimes he had been convicted of was life without parole.

At the hearing in the Federal District Court, Louima condemned Volpe's hints in the pre-trial hearings that his injuries were the result of homosexual activity, calling this 'an outrageous lie'. On being sentenced, Volpe said that his time with the NYPD had not been easy – 'I witnessed misery on a daily basis, I saw innocent babies dead, being handled like dead chickens in the morgue' – and that he and his colleagues had been assaulted and attacked by people that 'the rest of society doesn't even want to see'. He also expressed for the first time his apologies to Abner Louima. He also said, 'I hurt many people, I was and still am ashamed . . . I am extremely sorry, I must and I will pay for my crime.' Judge Nickerson was not impressed by this and told Volpe that his last-minute words of remorse were 'motivated by self-interest' and that his violence towards Louima had been 'a barbarous misuse of power'.

Rev. Al Sharpton told the media outside the courthouse that Volpe should have been given a life sentence. Volpe's father Robert said that the NYPD should be held accountable for what his son had done, and that psychological stress had paid its toll. Robert Volpe summarised: 'You can lose your life on that street, but you can also lose your soul.'

SCHWARZ, BRUDER AND WEISE TRIED FOR CONSPIRACY

In January 2000, jury selection started for the trial of officers Schwarz, Bruder and Weise on charges of conspiracy to obstruct justice by lying to investigators about the attack on Louima in the police building. On 3 January, outside the courthouse where the jury selection procedure was taking place, Rev. Al Sharpton said that this second trial was as important as the first, as 'what Justin Volpe did could not have been done without an active cover-up in the 70th Precinct.'

On 3 February 2000, the jury was finally chosen. On the first day of the trial on 7 February, Schwarz's attorney said that he planned to issue a subpoena on Justin Volpe in order to get him to testify of Schwarz's innocence. Lawyers for Bruder and Weise emphasised the good character of their clients. Appearing as a witness on 17 February, Volpe stated that Charles Schwarz took no part in any attack on Louima, but said that Officer Weise was present in the toilet and did nothing to stop Volpe from his brutal actions. Volpe also said that he had not always told the truth about what had happened: 'I lied to myself, I lied to my lawyer, I lied to my parents.'

Schwarz's lawyer Ronald Fischetti was pleased with Volpe's testimony but, despite this, on 7 March 2000 Schwarz, Bruder and Weise were found guilty of conspiracy to obstruct justice.

THE TRIAL OF FRANCISCO ROSARIO
On 5 June 2000, the trial of Officer Rosario opened at the Federal District Court in Brooklyn. It was alleged that Rosario had lied to investigators in initially denying that he had been in the 70th Precinct house during the attack on Louima. Another officer, Rolando Aleman, had pleaded guilty in April 2000 to the same charges Rosario now faced. Bizarrely, when questioned by Chief Prosecutor Alan Vinegrad, Rosario admitted that he had lied because he did not want to get a fellow officer into trouble. Not surprisingly, Rosario was found guilty on 21 June 2000. Neither officer was imprisoned; Aleman and Rosario were sentenced to two and three years of probation respectively.

SCHWARZ, BRUDER AND WEISE SENTENCED
On 28 June 2000, Schwarz's sentencing hearing took place. Before being sentenced, Schwarz told Judge Nickerson: 'I have no doubt in my mind that you will give me a harsh sentence. I refused to demean myself and beg for mercy for a crime I did not commit.' Schwarz's initial comment was correct – he was sentenced to fifteen years and eight months in prison for taking part in the attack on Louima and conspiring to cover up his guilt and that of other officers.

Louima told the press: 'I was hoping for the maximum sentence, but justice is served. It proves no one is above the law.' Thomas Bruder and Thomas Weise were sentenced to five years in prison for the offence of conspiracy. The three officers' attorney began to lodge appeals against their convictions.

LOUIMA'S LAWSUIT

On 22 March 2001, the New York City authorities and the New York Patrolmen's Benevolent Association proposed that they pay Louima a total of $8.75m as a settlement of his civil lawsuit – the $7m contributed by the city would be the largest amount ever paid out by them in a police brutality lawsuit. Mayor Giuliani said he hoped this would help the healing process in relations between the NYPD and black communities. After some legal wrangling, Louima accepted this sum – one-third of which would go to his attorneys – telling the press, 'I don't really see myself as a rich man, I see myself as someone who's lucky enough to be alive and able to see some justice.'

SCHWARZ'S LAWYERS MAKE BID FOR RETRIAL

In July 2001, a police officer who had interviewed Detective Turetzky at the 70th Precinct six days after the assault on Louima made contact with Charles Schwarz's lawyers, who moved to have the case against Schwarz retried, hoping for an acquittal.

In a formal affidavit the policeman, known as Officer F and later revealed as former Sergeant Patrick Walsh, gave testimony containing information that could overturn Schwarz's conviction. This affidavit contradicts Turetzky's account given to the court in which he described Officer Schwarz leading Abner Louima towards the Precinct toilet. On 15 August a hearing took place in the Federal District Court in Brooklyn, again before Judge Eugene Nickerson, in which Walsh and two other officers who had interviewed Turetzky, Captain James Peters and Sergeant Richard Tully, took the stand. Walsh and Peters told the Judge that Turetzky, when interviewed, had not been able to ascertain which officer had led Louima towards the toilet room.

Due to inaccuracies and contradictions in the three officers' testimonies, mainly that of Walsh who also confessed to the court that he had alcohol problems, Judge Nickerson rejected Schwarz's attorneys' plea for a retrial.

In February 2002, Schwarz filed papers from his prison cell accusing the Bureau of Prisons of keeping him in inhumane conditions. Due to the hostility by inmates and threats made to him, Schwarz was kept in what the authorities called 'administrative detention' for his own protection and moved from prison to prison. He alleged that he was kept in solitary confinement, allowed one hour of recreation per day and had to sleep on a concrete block.

SCHWARZ, WEISE AND BRUDER – CONVICTIONS OVERTURNED DUE TO INSUFFICIENT EVIDENCE

On 31 February 2002, the United States Court of Appeals made their decision regarding the appeals of Schwarz, Bruder and Weise against their original convictions on civil rights, assault and conspiracy charges. The Appeals Court found that prosecutors did not have enough evidence to secure convictions. They were also critical of Schwarz's attorney, Stephen Worth, and a possible conflict of interest as the law firm he worked for had frequently represented the NYPD. The convictions were thrown out, with a retrial ordered for Charles Schwarz. Rev. Al Sharpton called the court's ruling 'a shocking display of how the judicial system continues to fail to protect citizens against police abuse'. Abner Louima, who was now living in Miami Lakes, Florida, told reporters, 'I'm still in shock'. Bruder and Weise were freed hours after their convictions were quashed; on 7 March Charles Schwarz was freed on a $1m bond. A delighted Schwarz told the media today was 'a great day' as he was driven off to his mother's house in Staten Island.

In October 2002 Federal and State prosecutors announced that they would not be filing any additional charges against Weise or Bruder

RETRIAL OF CHARLES SCHWARZ

On 21 June 2002, the jury of ten men and two women assembled for the retrial of Schwarz for his part in the assault on Abner Louima and on charges of perjury. On 25 June, Louima took the stand in court and again described being beaten and then sodomised with a stick. He was questioned for several hours about the identity of the second officer in the toilet. On the following day, Sgt. Eric Turetzky told jurors, 'I observed Officer Schwarz take Mr Louima and escort him from the front desk area.' Turetzky also described seeing Schwarz push Louima towards the toilet where the assault took place. On 1 July, Justin Volpe was taken from prison to the courtroom where he was questioned as a witness for Schwarz's defence. Volpe told the court, 'Schwarz was never in the bathroom at any point.' Cross-examined by Chief Prosecutor Alan Vinegrad, Volpe was accused of testifying on behalf of Schwarz only in return for legal advice from Schwarz's attorneys. A taped prison phone-call from Volpe to his father was played to the jury in which Volpe said he was only helping Schwarz in order to get his jail sentence shortened. On 16 July, the jury found Schwarz guilty of perjury; they could not come to a majority verdict on the other charges.

SUBSEQUENT EVENTS

Two weeks after this retrial was concluded, the incoming US attorney for Brooklyn, Roslynnn Mauskopf, said that prosecutors could retry Schwarz yet again on the charges that the jury at the retrial were unable to reach a verdict on. On 20 September 2002 the jury was chosen, but this retrial was not to take place. In a deal between prosecutors and Judge Reena Raggi, Schwarz was given a five-year jail sentence for perjury. The remaining civil rights charges and another perjury charge were dropped.

In December 2002, it was reported that Thomas Weise and Thomas Bruder had applied for reinstatement in the NYPD, along with back pay from the date that they had been originally convicted.

IMPLICATIONS OF THE LOUIMA CASE

The attack on Louima increased racial tension in New York. The Haitian community, which had become cynical about whether American justice treated all races equally, was not surprised when many of the original convictions against the accused officers were quashed. The case is notable in that eventually the 'blue wall of silence' did break down as officers, for whatever motive, told authorities their versions of what had taken place. Despite this – and even though Abner Louima had ostensibly been able to identify this man – there was no conviction of the second officer for his part in the assault with the stick in the Precinct toilet. Hard evidence – such as forensically identifiable DNA or closed-circuit TV footage which would precisely identify who was involved in attacking Louima and at what time which officers were with him – was lacking in this case.

Volpe, now serving his thirty-year sentence, gave the explanation to the judge that the assault took place because he wanted to humiliate Louima. He also claimed that he had been psychologically influenced, having witnessed so much suffering and violence and having been on the receiving end of so much hostility during the course of his police career. Before the last word is spoken on the Louima case, the reasons for Volpe's behaviour, and that of the other officers who were either also involved in violence towards Louima or stood by, listening to his screams and doing nothing, deserve further explanation.

6. DENIS TANNER AND THE BONNIE DOON BODIES

John Harrison

Why is it that whenever a murder case emerges which involves a cross-gender victim, the story always seems to come across as so much more sordid and enticing? Are we that far desensitised to crime that only the addition of an exotic angle will pique our interest, or does it fascinate us because it indicates the work of a killer who has decidedly kinky proclivities along with a violent nature? When you throw an enigmatic, notorious policeman into this lethal mix, the cocktail becomes that much more exotic, dangerous and irresistible.

The Denis Tanner story is one of the most unusual and intriguing in modern Australian crime; one made even more mystifying by its eventual, unresolved outcome. In an age when police corruption and cover-ups are treated by many people as an ugly but inevitable part of the crime-fighting system, the name Denis Tanner still manages to invoke feelings of curiosity in many, and of sheer terror in a select few.

One of four brothers, Denis Tanner joined the Victorian Police Force on 22 October 1973, graduating from the Academy (22nd out of the 24 in his class) on 15 March 1974. A solid man with an intimidating demeanour, Tanner began active service at Russell Street, then spent time at South Melbourne and Shepparton, before finally being stationed at St Kilda. At the time (and even today, although to a lesser extent), St Kilda was one of the major hubs for Australia's drug and prostitution rackets, a beachfront suburb dominated by the infamous Fitzroy Street, whose string of skid-row pubs, grimy adult bookshops and neon-lit pinball parlours and fish and chip shops made it Melbourne's own miniature version of Los Angeles's infamous Sunset Strip (unfortunately, it has now become a haven for yuppies, with pretentious coffee houses and overpriced department stores).

Although Tanner was apparently counselled by officers in the 1970s for not following proper procedures, on 4 May 1978 he received a commendation, alongside three other officers, for his dedication to duty and courage, and for the valour which he displayed in the apprehension of a violent criminal.

On 14 May 1978 Denis Tanner arrested Adele Bailey, a New Zealand born transsexual working the streets of St Kilda, on charges of loitering for prostitution and homosexual purposes. A heavy drug user with rumoured connections to the underworld, Bailey had arrived in Australia in the early 1970s, working the streets while trying to save up the $2000 needed for her sex change operation, which she had done on the cheap in Europe (where you didn't have to undergo a battery of psychological tests or live as a woman for a certain amount of time). It was after her return to Australia that Bailey began to migrate to the St Kilda area, becoming a well-known figure to many of the local cops who patrolled the streets.

When Bailey failed to turn up to her court appearance on 15 September 1978, and when Tanner issued a warrant for her arrest a month later, she had simply vanished from the face of the earth. Her flatmate had arrived home to find the front door ajar and Adele nowhere to be seen.

While Adele Bailey's family and friends undertook a frustrating and fruitless search for answers, Denis

Tanner continued his impressive climb up the police ladder, being transferred to the CIB in 1979, and promoted to the rank of senior detective, working in the Major Crime squad.

In 1981 Denis's brother Laurie married Jennifer Blake, with Denis signing the marriage certificate. Although he could never have foreseen it at the time, the marriage would be the seed that would lead to Denis Tanner's eventual downfall and disgrace as a police officer.

Three years after the wedding, on 14 November 1984, Jennifer Tanner's body was discovered in the living room of their farmhouse in the Victorian country town of Bonnie Doon, slumped over her husband's bolt-action .22-calibre rifle. She had been shot twice in the head, as well as through both hands (which usually indicates the victim had been in a defensive position). Her infant son was discovered unharmed in the bedroom, sleeping peacefully.

The two country police officers who were called to the scene were confronted with the site of Jennifer Tanner's body slumped on the couch, rifle propped between her knees, the barrel pointed into her profusely bleeding head (Laurie Tanner claimed that when he found his wife's body he didn't notice the bullet holes through both hands).

The death of Jennifer Tanner was extremely suspect from the outset. The police at the scene decided to call in Alexandra-based Ian Welsh; however, the Detective Sergeant, known as 'Columbo' to the locals, decided against visiting the crime scene to personally investigate, even after he was informed of the discovery of a second bullet cartridge lying near the body. Incredibly, Welsh also decided that fingerprinting, photographs and forensic tests were not necessary (Welsh would deny ever having received the initial telephone call at the 1997 inquest into Jennifer's death).

While suicide was to be the initial consensus in the death of Jennifer Tanner, Bill Kerr, the older of the two constables who had been first on the scene (Don Frazer being his partner), harboured a number of serious doubts, which he kept to himself for a number of years. Kerr – well aware that Jennifer was the sister-in-law of Denis Tanner – wondered about the cup of coffee and plate of biscuits that were sitting next to Jennifer's body, and why she would leave her baby alone in another room. The position of the body also troubled him, along with the bloodstains on the couch. It almost seemed as if the body had been lying down at some point, before being propped up in a seated position.

There was also no suicide note and, as the two officers made the trip to break the news to Jennifer Tanner's parents, Kerr noted a police radio message, which revealed that Denis Tanner was not at his Footscray apartment when Melbourne police arrived to see him.

Amazingly, the morning after Jennifer's death, another of Denis Tanner's brothers, Bruce Frederick, was allowed to enter the farmhouse and clean up the site of the apparent suicide, potentially erasing evidence at a possible crime scene. The initial inquest into Jennifer Tanner's death was held in late 1995 and, although some fingers and whispers of suspicions were clearly directed at Denis Tanner (he was represented by well-known attorney Joe Gullaci),[1] the police's handling of the death was considered so botched that the laying of any murder charges was considered impossible, with an open finding being the verdict of the inquest.

Controversy continued to dog Denis Tanner throughout the latter half of the 80s. In March 1988, he was believed to be responsible for selling information to big-time drug dealers William Hackett and Terrance Moon, who were the focus of a major undercover investigation into an amphetamines distribution ring (which police had dubbed Operation Mint). It is claimed that Tanner received vital information regarding the operation from a drug squad officer who worked at the same building, then used a former policeman to pass the details on to Hackett and Moon. (In October 1989, the detective suspected of leaking news to Tanner resigned six weeks after being questioned on the matter by Chief Inspector Tony Warren.)

Denis Tanner transferred to the country town of Benalla in December 1988, holding the rank of detective sergeant (his wife, also in the police force, resigned from her position at the Altona station in order to be with him). It wasn't long after the move that Tanner was being counselled by his superiors at Benalla, for using inappropriate language.

The following February, Tanner seriously hurt his knee during a vicious struggle with a criminal in the Benalla cells. Two months later, he requested forty days leave to recover from stress and anxiety, no doubt brought on by the growing widespread allegations that he was suspected of serious corruption.

Upon Tanner's return to duty in June 1989, he was interviewed by investigators in relation to Operation Mint, and was later informed by Police Commissioner Neil Comrie that Command intended to demote him to the Police Reserve, which eventuated in January of 1990, after Deputy Commissioner Brendan Crimmins wrote a letter to Denis Tanner in regard to Operation Mint, in which he clearly branded Tanner a crook. Tanner immediately appealed the transfer.

Tanner's appeal to the Police Services Board was heard by former Police Commander Eric Sutton, former policeman Fred Leslie and County Court Judge Walsh. The appeal – in which eleven serving and former police, ranked from constable to chief inspector, told the hearing that Tanner was a valuable and trusted member of the CIB – was successful, and his transfer to the Police Reserves was overturned. The Services Board believed that there were clear indications of corruption in Operation Mint, but Tanner's link to any of them could not be proved.

THE FARM GIVES UP ITS SECRETS

On 20 July 1995, Mick Bladen and his friend Dave Worsley, Melbourne residents who frequently journeyed to Bonnie Doon for campouts and mountain climbing treks, were returning from a day's exploring when they came upon the old, and long disused, Jack o' Clubs mineshaft, situated on a property not far from the farmhouse where Jennifer Tanner died. Named after the unknown original owner of the mine – because of his skill at playing blackjack – the mine yielded fine, rich concentrations of gold in the late-1800s, but had been long since tapped out and abandoned, a large cherry tree growing by the entrance its only companion.

On a whim, Bladen and Worsley decided to venture down the mineshaft, descending via a rope tied to the cherry tree. What they found down there was not what they had expected. Reaching the first level ten metres down, Worsley shone his torch down on to the next level of the shaft and, with a sudden wave of fear surging through him, solved a 17-year-old mystery. Adele Bailey had been found.

The partially clothed skeleton was wearing lingerie, high-heeled boots and jewellery. Although the remains were too old to establish a definite cause of death, a number of Bailey's bones were broken, and several police officers privately revealed to author Robin Bowles (see Bibliography) that Adele had probably been either kicked to death or 'copped the chicken' (a police slang term for almost choking someone to death, then letting them go from a height).

Tanner's clear link to Bailey,[2] combined with Andrew Rule's[3] article in the Sunday 9 June 1996 edition of the *Sunday Age* (which probed the inconsistencies surrounding Jennifer Tanner's supposed suicide), led to the original inquest into Jennifer's death being quashed, and the re-opening of a new inquiry, which was designated Operation Kale.

Less than two months after the mineshaft discovery, the old Tanner homestead – which had been sold shortly after Jennifer's death to an absentee owner – mysteriously burnt to the ground. The fire began outside and engulfed the building before firefighters could arrive. Any DNA or forensic evidence which may have been recovered was gone for good.

The new inquest into the murder of Jennifer Tanner began in October 1997. In his opening address, Jeremy Rapke made public for the first time the name of Sergeant Helen Golding. It was revealed that Golding, godmother to Denis Tanner's children, and formerly his wife's best friend, had received a series of death threats. When Golding herself appeared in the courtroom a week later, she looked stressed out and visibly nervous, and a weapon check had been conducted on everyone who entered the court.

Golding revealed to the court that she had contacted the Jennifer Tanner taskforce in October 1996, after reading the *Sunday Age* piece. Since giving a statement about Denis Tanner to detectives, she had not been able to sleep properly, and had been too scared to even walk her dog or ride her horse alone. She had also received a number of disturbing, and none too subtle, messages through the mail. She was sent a dagger (covered in fake blood), leaflets from funeral homes, a sympathy card with 'you're dead' written on it, a .22 calibre bullet, and a wreath with the message 'Time Runs Out', which was left on her front doorstep. She also received a letter containing her current work roster, with the words 'I miss you' inscribed on it.

Bill Kerr, the constable who kept his suspicions to himself when first called to the scene on the night of Jennifer Tanner's death, was also called to the stand. Kerr told the court that he had believed Jennifer Tanner was murdered ever since the autopsy two days after her death showed that she had two bullets in her skull, as well as bullet wounds in each hand. Kerr also recalled his claims that he had called detective Ian Welsh to inform him of irregularities at the scene, only to be told by Welsh to continue to treat the investigation as a suicide, and not to gather evidence as if it were a crime scene. Kerr also said he had become frustrated by his superiors, who repeatedly denied his requests for forensic tests on the rifle, and for a list of questions to be put to Denis Tanner. He also expressed his curiosity when he heard the radio report revealing that Tanner had not been at home when police called in shortly after the discovery of Jennifer's body.

(Denis Tanner's wife Lynn claimed that her husband did not return home until early morning on the night Jennifer died. After initially claiming that he had been at the horse races at the time of the death, Tanner changed his story months later, telling homicide detective Albert Fry that he had been providing security at a bingo night in the inner Melbourne suburb of Albert Park. Tanner was never officially questioned over his change of alibi, despite the fact that the race meeting which he originally claimed to be at had not even taken place on the same night as Jennifer Tanner's death.)

Don Frazer, the constable who accompanied Kerr to the Tanner home, told the coroner he regretted the way things were handled on the night Jennifer Tanner was shot (he had progressed to the position of sergeant by the time he faced the inquiry).

Superintendent Peter Fleming – who would later join the anti-corruption unit – assisted the coroner in the 1985 autopsy of Jennifer Tanner. Fleming testified that he felt the investigation of Jennifer's death was inadequate at every level, adding that he had been concerned that nothing was being done to rectify it. He recalled a heated meeting with homicide squad officers where Albert Fry seemed adamant that the death was a suicide, and was supported by his superiors, who refused to investigate the matter.

Bruce Frederick Tanner, who appeared to be tense and borderline aggressive throughout his time on the stand, explained his own curious behaviour in the immediate aftermath of Jennifer's death. His version of events were that his mother had telephoned him at around 6 a.m. with the bad news. Setting off to Mansfield to comfort his parents (as well as brother Laurie), Bruce Tanner decided to stop off at the farmhouse where the shooting had occurred, where he went in and cleaned up the grisly aftermath. When asked why he did this, rather than head straight to his grieving family, Bruce explained that a policeman had claimed that his mother would be expected to clean up the scene, and he was not prepared to let her suffer through that. Unfortunately, he was unable to recollect the name of the police officer who had given him this information.

Leaving the court with his family after his day on the stand, Bruce Tanner was walking to his car when his brother Denis swung his briefcase into the groin of a *Herald-Sun* photographer. As he drove away, Bruce Tanner flung the door to his car open, knocking the same photographer to the ground.

Among the other statements given during the hearing was that of the doctor who performed the initial autopsy on Jennifer Tanner's body, who admitted that he tried at the time to make the two head wounds, as well as the two wounds on the hands, fit the police's dogged opinion that the death was a suicide.

Coroner Graeme Johnstone delivered his finding into the 1984 death of Jennifer Tanner on 10 December 1998, stating that she had been killed by her brother-in-law, Detective Sergeant Denis Tanner. The courtroom sat galvanised as Johnstone told them that Denis shot her at least three times with her husband's bolt-action .22 rifle.

Despite the finding – along with the public outrage and damning media coverage which followed it – charges were not laid against Denis Tanner. It seemed obvious that much of the evidence considered by Johnstone would be inadmissible in a criminal trial, and with no eyewitnesses and any forensic evidence long since destroyed, there would be insufficient substantiation to put Tanner before a jury.

Still, the findings had highlighted the gross ineptitude of the initial handling of Jennifer Tanner's death, and put the heat of the spotlight clearly on Denis Tanner. For the media and news-hungry public, it was also an enthralling curtain-raiser to the forthcoming inquest into the death of Adele Bailey, which finally got underway in early 1999.

At the Bailey inquest, one of the most damning statements was that of a former insurance clerk, Mrs Janine Fletcher, who claimed that Mark O'Loughlin, a former client, policeman and friend of Denis Tanner, had boasted of the parties which had taken place at his holiday home at Bonnie Doon, where prostitutes and strippers were taken along. Fletcher also overheard O'Loughlin talking about how the police would regularly let the transsexual prostitutes get roughed up by the men in their holding cells.

Fletcher further identified Denis Tanner as having the same eyes as a policeman who had pulled her over in her car and threatened her after she had questioned her employer over a suspicious insurance claim lodged by O'Loughlin. Fletcher said she processed three insurance claims for Mark O'Loughlin with insurance broker Complete Financial Services in the early 1980s. One of the claims was for cash and a large amount of alcohol stolen from O'Loughlin's Bonnie Doon holiday house.

The claim which forced Mrs Fletcher to raise her suspicions was for the theft of jewellery from O'Loughlin's car. When she noticed a similar lot of jewellery being advertised for sale in *The Trading Post*, Fletcher called the number listed in the ad, only to find it being answered by the South Melbourne police station where O'Loughlin was based. Fletcher's boss, Denis Jones, told her to back off when she pointed out the advertisement to him (Jones kept a number of police officers on his books as clients).

A week after raising the issue with her boss, Mrs Fletcher was pulled up by a plain-clothes policeman, whom she later identified as Denis Tanner. Fletcher told the court that Tanner told her in no uncertain terms to keep her nose out of other people's business, and to leave his friends alone. Fletcher, whose confrontation with Tanner left her rattled and scared, later received a number of threatening telephone calls. She eventually decided to contact police after reading the 1996 article on the Tanner case in the *Sunday Age*.

Unlike the Jennifer Tanner inquest, the Adele Bailey hearing was relatively short. Because of the age of the crime, and the lack of any useable, concrete evidence, Coroner Jacinta Heffey was left with no choice but to make an open finding.

Not long after the Bailey hearing – on 28 July 1999 – Denis Tanner resigned from the police force. He escaped having any murder charges laid against him after senior prosecutors informed the Victorian Director of Public Prosecutions that there was no reasonable prospect of obtaining a conviction. He was last known to be working as a cab driver.

On 13 March 2002, John Silvester reported in *The Age* that Chief Commissioner Christine Nixon had called in the federal police to investigate a claim of perjury against Victorian police officers on the murder taskforce that investigated Denis Tanner over the murder of Jennifer Tanner and the death of Adele Bailey.

The federal police were particularly interested in the taskforce's decision to place listening devices in the house of a serving policeman, Senior Detective Gerry McHugh. It is alleged that Senior Detective McHugh may have been at a party with Denis Tanner at Bonnie Doon, where Adele Bailey either overdosed and died, or was killed, in 1978. The Supreme Court granted a warrant to install listening devices in McHugh's Mildura home. McHugh, a policeman with more than 25 years' experience, later found the devices. Subsequent investigations found that McHugh was not at the Bonnie Doon party and was not involved with Adele Bailey's disappearance.

A FATAL LINK?

Was there a connection between Jennifer Tanner and Adele Bailey, a link which would bind these two very different personalities together in the cold, black void of death? Nothing points to the pair ever having met in life – the most popular explanation would seem to be that Jennifer Tanner had the misfortune to stumble upon the secret of what lay in that abandoned mineshaft out the back of her property, and either threatened to talk or was silenced before she ever had the chance to do so.

Another popular theory bandied about suggested that the murders of Jennifer Tanner and Adele Bailey were completely unrelated (save for the likelihood that they were committed by the same person), that Jennifer was killed because she was unhappy with her marriage and planning to divorce her husband, and someone was not prepared to see part of the family assets handed over to her (Laurie Tanner had already been through one very costly divorce with his first wife, Sally).

Of course, this is all now just a matter of speculation and, although we have many of the individual pieces, it seems highly unlikely that we will ever view the complete picture. When one drives through the outskirts of Bonnie Doon – about two hours out of Melbourne – it is easy to be convinced of a strange eeriness, and feeling of foreboding, that hangs in the air. It is not so much a feeling of current danger, more the echo of an evil, one that's all too human, that once pervaded the farmlands. It provides a grim reminder that horror can indeed lurk within serenity and beauty, and the evils of crime and corruption can spread its wings far beyond the claustrophobic, dirty confines of the metropolis.

And somewhere out there, another killer has gotten away with murder.

BIBLIOGRAPHY

Robin Bowles, *Blind Justice*, St Leonards: Allen & Unwin, 1998.
Robin Bowles, *No Justice*, Sydney: Macmillan, 2000.

A Note on the Bibliography

Robin Bowles was a Melbourne company director with very little in the way of investigative writing experience, when she opened up the 9 June 1996 edition of the *Sunday Age* and read the report on the new police probe into Jennifer Tanner's death.

Deeply affected by the story, Bowles decided that Jennifer Tanner would be the perfect subject for her long-planned first book, and almost overnight she closed up her company and concentrated all of her time and resources into investigating Jennifer's life and the mystery surrounding her death. The result was *Blind Justice*, a thorough and riveting examination of the case (and one which won her quite a number of enemies, both during its writing and after publication).

A critical and commercial success, *Blind Justice* led Bowles to further examine the Adele Bailey case, which was the subject of her third book, *No Justice* (Bowles's second book, *Justice Denied*, looked at the unsolved murder of Moe toddler Jaidyn Leskie in 1997).

Of Bowles's two books which delve into the world of Dennis Tanner, *No Justice* is the most intriguing and memorable of the two, giving not only a complete biography of Adele Bailey (including the fruitless efforts of her loved ones to locate her after her disappearance), but also effectively bringing back to life the sordid world of 1970s vice in which both Bailey and Denis Tanner operated. *No Justice* also gives the reader an interesting window into Melbourne's transgender culture during this period, tracking down and interviewing a number of the transsexuals with whom Adele Bailey associated during her time in Melbourne (as well as in Sydney's notorious Kings Cross).

NOTES
1. A short but tough man with a gravelly voice and the required penchant for courtroom drama, Joe Gullaci's reputation helped him win both high-profile policemen and organised crime figures as clients. At his first trial in 1973, he represented a transsexual prostitute, Vicky Liddy, who had attacked a customer with a broken bottle after he refused to pay up. Although Liddy was found guilty, Gullaci was able to win her a greatly reduced sentence, and he quickly graduated from representing prostitutes and low-rent drug dealers to defending some of the country's biggest criminal cases, including that of Raymond Patrick Bennet, the mastermind behind the 1976 Great Bookie Robbery (where six gunmen robbed millions of dollars from bookmakers at the Victorian Club). When Bennet was shot outside a courtroom in 1979, by a hit man disguised as a lawyer, Gullaci pushed Bennet's wife Gail out of the line of fire, then later took her to hospital to visit her fatally injured husband. Joe Gullaci was appointed a County Court judge in June 2002.
2. Throughout the early 1980s, most police department watch house books – large, cumbersome leather-bound volumes – were destroyed to make way for shelf space as computerised systems slowly took over. For historical purposes, a select few of the old volumes were kept for display in the Police Museum. Ironically, some of the books kept were the St Kilda police station volumes from October 1976 to January 1979, which contained complete records of Adele

Bailey's arrests during that time. The records showed that Bailey had been arrested by Tanner, which in itself was not uncommon as it would have been part of Tanner's job tasks at the time, but it did provide Operation Kale investigators with clear proof that Bailey and Tanner were known to each other.

3. A senior reporter for *The Age* – specialising in stories on crime and corruption – Andrew Rule was one of the most prominent journalists attached to the Denis Tanner investigation. His 1996 *Sunday Age* piece on the inconsistencies of the initial Jennifer Tanner death enquiry helped pave the way for the new inquest, and many of the people who decided to testify at the subsequent inquests into both Jennifer Tanner and Adele Bailey claim they decided to come forward after reading Rule's article. (While research-ing the piece, two heavy roof tiles were thrown through the window of Rule's car as it was parked outside his home.) A recipient of the 1996 Australian Journalist of the Year award, Rule has also written on the Port Arthur Massacre, and has penned (with John Silvester) the popular series of *Underbelly* books, published by Sly Ink, which chronicle true Austra-lian crime cases. Rule also narrated a 1996 television documentary on the Denis Tanner case.

7. DEATH UNDER THE INFLUENCE

JOSEPH GRAY VS. THE HERRERA FAMILY
Mikita Brottman

After the events of September 11 2001, it seemed as though the New York Police Department could do no wrong. In the Big Apple, police officers, like firefighters, had suddenly become idols and superheroes, their bravery and selflessness matters of national pride. NYPD baseball caps, T-shirts, badges and flags lined the shelves of souvenir stores all over the city. But not all NYPD officers had such an upstanding reputation. Even after September 11, many New Yorkers could not forget the case of Joseph Gray, and were determined that this killer cop should be held accountable for his crimes.

Officer Joseph Gray, a tall, middle-aged, distinguished-looking man with a dark moustache and salt-and-pepper hair, was at one time known as the 'Prince of the 72nd Precinct,' the Brooklyn neighbourhood in which he'd lived and worked for his entire life. A family man, he had three daughters at home – one from his wife's previous marriage – and had an exemplary record with the NYPD.

Like many policemen, however, Officer Gray had a major vice: he was no stranger to the bottle.

On the night of Friday 3 August 2001, Joe Gray was, as usual, working the graveyard shift at the 72nd Precinct, dealing with the drunks and derelicts who were brought into the station throughout the night. It was a fairly uneventful evening, and the night passed in routine police work until the next shift came on duty at 8 a.m. the following morning, Saturday 4 August. It was at this remarkably early hour that Joe Gray and his fellow officers started their day-long drinking binge.

It was a hot August morning, and Officer Gray and his hard-drinking pals popped open their first few beers in the parking lot of the Precinct stationhouse in Brooklyn. Among the officer's boozing buddies that morning were John Welsh and Craig Hildebrand – both probationary officers with less than two years on the job – and Edward Sills, a policeman who was on disciplinary probation for a drunk-driving infraction within the last year. It wasn't unusual for these party cops to sit drinking in the Precinct parking lot – in fact, it happened all the time. They'd even made themselves a makeshift urinal out of the fence and guttering on one side of the car park.

That morning was the beginning of a kind of informal stag party – one of the officers, Sgt. Dennis Healey, was to be married the following day. The men started their celebrations that morning and, in the best police tradition, were planning to keep drinking as long and as hard as they possibly could. At some point in the early afternoon, the party of boozy cops drove into Brooklyn and reconvened at a local strip club, The Wild, Wild West. This club, which used to be the self-proclaimed 'home of the $10 lap dance' (but has apparently since raised the price to $20), is part of a cluster of sex-related businesses on the waterfront of Brooklyn's Sunset Park, and offers free lunch and a free after-work buffet to entice potential customers. However, The Wild, Wild West was supposed to be off-limits to the cops from the 72nd Precinct, since it was part of the same neighbourhood they were charged with protecting, and known to be 'corruption-prone'.

At the club, Gray apparently spent most of his time talking to a stripper called Chastity Jenkins. Chastity claimed that the policeman had confessed to her that he was utterly miserable, that he hated his wife, and that he hated being married. She said he was so drunk that he passed out two or three times at the bar, and she had to keep waking him up. Around 3.30 that afternoon, Joe Gray took the bridegroom-to-be Dennis Healey back to his truck in the Precinct parking lot, where the two cops sat talking and drinking for about an hour. Gray then drove back to the strip club.

Nobody knows exactly how much Joe Gray actually drank before returning home that afternoon but, despite his boasts about his tolerance for alcohol, he was definitely a few sheets to the wind. He later admitted to consuming at least twelve beers; others claim it must have been at least eighteen. The carefree cop had been drinking all day, without a break, from eight o'clock in the morning until it was time for him to go back to work again at nine o'clock that night. When he set off back to the 72nd precinct in his family minivan for another stint on the graveyard shift, the partying policeman hadn't slept in over 24 hours, and had spent the last thirteen of those hours drinking. It seems fairly safe to speculate that he was totally wrecked.

Meanwhile, elsewhere in Brooklyn, a heavily pregnant 24-year-old Dominican woman named Maria Herrera was just setting off on the short walk to her mother's apartment building, accompanied by her 4-year-old son Andy, and sixteen-year-old sister, Dilcia Pena. The family had just returned from a shopping trip to Sears, and Maria wanted to show her mother the baby clothes she had bought. Only a month away from giving birth, she found it tough to walk far in the August heat but, in this case, she didn't have a long way to go. Her mother lived nearby, in the shadow of the Gowanus Expressway, just two blocks from the East River.

It was a humid night. As usual, Maria and the kids walked to the crosswalk at the intersection of Third

Avenue and 46th Street in Sunset Park and stood waiting for the lights to change. When the 'walk' sign came on, the family stepped out into the road.

Suddenly, out of nowhere, Joseph Gray's speeding 1996 Ford Windstar hurtled around the corner, sped straight through the red light of the crossing and ploughed directly into the entire family, knocking them off their feet. The force of the crash threw bodies, footwear, baby clothes and shopping bags all over the road, with some items being hurled a distance of almost 128 feet. Gray immediately jammed on his brakes, bringing his vehicle to a sudden, screeching halt. The crash was so dramatic that his airbag deployed, and it took him a few minutes to extract himself from the front seat and get out of the car. When he did so, he was confronted with the sight of two women, one of them heavily pregnant, lying in a mangled heap in the road. Blood seeping from underneath his car revealed the fact that another child was pinned underneath his vehicle.

But the party cop did nothing.

'You've got a four-year-old boy under your car and you're a trained police officer and you do nothing to help?' asked the indignant prosecuting attorney in court.

'No,' said Gray, shaking his head. 'When I saw the condition, I knew there was nothing I could do.'

There were a number of witnesses to the accident, and Gray began shouting for somebody to call 911 immediately. As officers began to arrive at the scene from his own precinct, the 72nd, a crowd of neighbourhood residents started to gather. Freddie Roman, a local man whose backyard overlooked the crosswalk, ran up to Gray, who seemed to be standing there in shock, and started shaking him, trying to alert him to the seriousness of the accident.

'He seemed like he was drunk,' said Roman. 'I told him, "Look what you did, look what you did!" He just said, "Come on, man, we all have a few beers once in a while." '

When the ambulance arrived, the limp bodies of the two women were covered with sheets and removed from the scene. The child was extracted from underneath Gray's vehicle and also taken to hospital. Sixteen-year-old Dilcia Pena was killed at the scene of the accident. Maria Herrera and her four-year-old son Andy were taken to Lutheran Medical Center, where Andy died about an hour after the accident. Before she died, Maria's baby was delivered by Caesarian section and the newborn baby boy, christened Ricardo Nicanor, was transferred to the Columbia Presbyterian Medical Center.

Back at the scene of the crash, Joe Gray was led into a patrol car belonging to a police colleague from the 72nd Precinct, Captain Bryan White – an old buddy of his from high school. Gray seemed relieved that the officer responding to the accident was his longtime pal.

'Just between me and you, Joe,' said Captain White in the squad car, 'I have to know if you've been drinking.'

Gray admitted that yes, he might have had one or two. 'I'm glad it's someone like you, Bryan,' he told his friend. 'I know I'll get a fair shake. I had green lights all the way. I've got to admit I was drinking, but it was earlier. I was on my way to work and they darted in front of me. I didn't see them coming.'

This 'squad car confessional,' during which the guilty cop apparently sucked compulsively on breath mints, later proved controversial in court, when Gray attacked his pal for airing what he'd assumed was a private conversation between two old friends. 'Had I known that Captain White's questions constituted an interrogation, I wouldn't have responded to any questions about drinking that day,' Gray said later.

The two officers drove back together to the 72nd precinct, where Joseph Gray was offered a breathalyser and co-ordination tests by Officer Martin Finkelstein, another old friend, both of which he declined to take. What happened next proved highly controversial in court. Apparently, Martin Finkelstein and Joe Gray telephoned three different friends – members of the Patrolman's Benevolent Association – in order to discuss ways in which the addled cop could beat the alcohol tests. 'Thinking back to the time, my intention was to give the subject a benefit,' confessed Officer Finkelstein in court. He has since 'retired' from the force.

As a result of these delaying tactics, Joe Gray's blood alcohol content was not measured until over four hours after the accident, at which time it proved to be 0.16, still way above the legal limit for New York of 0.10. According to experts, a driver with a blood alcohol level of 0.16 is 25 times more likely than a sober driver to be involved in an accident. Apparently, Gray's blood alcohol content four hours earlier, at the time of the crash, could have been as high as 0.22. It was estimated that he'd had to have consumed at least of 11 cans of beer to get a 0.16 reading four hours later, but that he'd probably drunk a whole lot more than that.

The day after the accident, 5 August 2001, baby Ricardo Nicanor Herrera died in his father's arms after spending twelve hours on a life support machine. He was buried in his mother's coffin. The same day, Joseph Gray was suspended from the NYPD and arraigned in Brooklyn Criminal Court for manslaughter, driving while intoxicated, and a series of other minor charges. Despite the prosecutor's request for $500,000 bail, the judge decided to release Officer Gray on his own recognisance.

The decision to release Gray was publicly denounced the following day by Rudolph Guiliani, the Mayor of New York City, after it sparked a collective outrage in the largely working-class immigrant community of Sunset Park. Three days after the killing, a group of almost a thousand residents marched to the 72nd precinct en masse, bearing picket signs and wielding megaphones. Led by Maria Herrera's grieving husband Victor, the crowd shouted chants of 'No Justice, No Peace,' and Victor Herrera spoke eloquently of his anguish. 'I am here with a picture of my family that has been taken away by a cop driving drunk,' he shouted to the crowd. 'Justice for me is to see him in prison, to see him in prison to pay for what he did.'

On 8 August, in response to this public outcry, seventeen cops at the 72nd Precinct were either disciplined, transferred to desk duty, or suspended without pay, including the commanding officer. All seventeen policemen were accused of abusing alcohol and either condoning or participating in the precinct's 'party atmosphere'. New rules were introduced that meant officers on disciplinary probation could no longer work the night shift. On 9 August, a grand jury indicted Joseph Gray for three counts each of manslaughter and vehicular manslaughter – one charge each for Maria Herrera, Dilcia Pena and Andy Herrera – as well as driving under the influence, reckless driving, reckless endangerment, speeding and disobeying a red light. Arraigned in Brooklyn Supreme Court on the indictment, Gray posted bail – this time set at $250,000 – and was released, pending trial. Protesters rallied outside the courtroom during the proceedings.

On the following day, 9 August, three of Gray's drinking pals were fired from the NYPD in connection with the incident. Edward Sills, an eighteen-year veteran of the force, was given the boot, along with the two hard-drinking rookies John Welsh and Craig Hildebrand. Mayor Guiliani announced that these suspensions 'should send a very clear message that drinking and being a police officer is a very dangerous combination'. And in case anyone else accused the NYPD of being soft on its own, on 14 August the police force slapped Gray with additional departmental charges, including manslaughter, possessing and consuming alcohol in a police parking lot and drinking alcohol inside an off-limits location. Two weeks later, under great pressure and with a trial looming, Officer Joseph Gray resigned from the NYPD.

In September, Joe Gray was indicted on an additional manslaughter charge for the death of Ricardo Herrera, Maria Herrera's unborn child. Despite the defence's argument that the unborn child was 'not a "person" as contemplated in the homicide statute,' the judge decided that if Gray killed the mother, he'd killed the unborn child as well. Public outrage continued in the build-up to the trial. The Rev. Al Sharpton led a march to the intersection where the fatal crash occurred, and when Gray held a press conference to apologise for the incident, it was interrupted by an activist screaming 'No bail for drunken killer cops!'

The trial was set for August 2002. Although the events of September 11 revitalised the status of police officers in New York, public sentiment was stacked sharply against Gray, who was painted in the press as a boozing, irresponsible killer. The case became a focal point for anti-police activists after reports of the cops' drinking became public, and many saw the case as yet another example of police brutality against powerless immigrants, the kind of behaviour that galvanised public opinion against the police in the recent Diallo and Louima cases.

When the trial began, it was clear that the defence didn't really have much of a case. Joseph Gray's attorney, Harold Levy, argued that his client was simply proceeding at the speed limit through a green light, when the family 'darted out' into the road in front of him. Levy made the case that Gray's view of the pedestrian crossing was hampered by the dim light of the expressway, as well as an array of construction barrels in the left lane. 'Joe Gray didn't do much to be proud of that day,' said Levy, but went on to argue that although the cop was legally intoxicated, it wasn't drunk driving that caused the collision, since Gray had a higher alcohol tolerance than most people. Levy pointed out that Officer Gray had visited three ATMs that day, taking out a total of $400, and didn't seem to have any problems operating them or remembering his PIN number.

In his defence of Joseph Gray, Levy tried to paint a more sober picture of the officer by showing jurors a tape made at the 72nd Precinct, where Gray was brought for the breathalyser and co-ordination tests after the accident. In the three-minute segment, which was played in court, Gray stood stock still and seemed to be pretty much in control of himself. The defence also emphasised Gray's record on the force. At one point, he'd apparently received a police award when he and a partner apprehended a murder suspect who'd just attempted to kill someone else. On another occasion, he'd captured six armed gang members who were headed to Manhattan to retaliate against another gang.

Levy argued that 'you should judge a man by his character, not just by this one action.' He told the jury that Gray was basically a good cop and a family man, with a perfect record in his police work. He also pointed out that Gray's family and friends had sent over 100 letters to the court begging that he be shown leniency. 'For fourteen years I have been a good citizen,' Gray told the judge, 'and I have never done anything intentionally wrong.' He then made an impassioned apology to the family of the victims.

Lawyers for the prosecution clearly had their work cut out for them. Witnesses to the crash included Mauro Giraldo and Angel LaFarge, two men who claimed that Gray's van was travelling at about 45 miles per hour. Another witness claimed that the traffic light was quite clearly red and the pedestrian 'walk' signal flashing as the victims entered the crossing. An accident reconstruction expert and two medical examiners testified that the victims all had to have come from Gray's right, giving him five seconds to have seen them on the pedestrian crossing. The prosecution ridiculed Levy's argument that this mother and two children had 'hurled themselves' in front of the policeman's vehicle.

Prosecutor Joseph Petrosino asked the judge for the maximum sentence for Gray, on the grounds that the former cop 'did what he did because he thought he could'. 'He basically did what he wanted,' said Petrosino. 'He thought he could rule over the neighbourhood.'

Maureen McCormick, another prosecuting attorney, took issue with the defence's description of Joseph Gray as a 'devoted family man'. 'The bottom line here is that he spent the entire day drinking while his wife and kids were home on a Saturday,' she argued. 'This devoted family man spent his day drinking, spending the family money and talking to a woman whose name he can't even remember.'

'He's a disgrace to the New York City Police Department,' said McCormick. 'He may wish to believe that this crash happened the way he said it did. But wishes don't change facts. If they did, then these people would still be alive.' She concluded with an emotional appeal to the jury for justice, pulling a torn, tan blouse out of an evidence bag and pointing to a pair of handbags found at the scene. 'All that is left is these blood-soiled clothes,' she said.

On 13 August 2002, ex-Officer Joseph Gray was convicted of four charges of second-degree manslaughter and sentenced to the maximum term, five to fifteen years in prison. 'He tempted fate by driving a thousand pounds of metal through the populated streets of Brooklyn,' said the judge. 'While I want to be merciful and humane, I also want to impose a sentence that will address the crime committed.'

Before his sentence was decided, the victims' family, who'd recently filed a petition with over a thousand names requesting that the binge-drinking cop be given the maximum sentence, was given a chance to explain their grief to the judge. 'Anger consumes me,' said Maria Herrera's husband Victor. 'This is what has become of my life. I have nothing.' He almost broke down in tears when he told the court that he'd offered to go with his wife on that fateful day, but she said he should stay at home and rest, because the baby could be coming at any time.

Maria Herrera's mother, Maria Pena, was overcome by grief and unable to speak at the trial, so her sister, Ramona Hernandez, spoke for her. 'These people were full of life,' she said, holding up pictures of the victims. 'Ricardo didn't even get to see the sunlight.'

After the trial and sentencing were over, relatives of the victims filed two civil suits totalling $300 million, charging the police department with being soft on alcoholic cops. The first suit, filed on 14 August 2002, claimed that there was a party atmosphere at the 72nd Precinct, and that 'such an atmosphere fostered the belief in alcohol-abusing police officers that they were insulated from discipline, investigation, prosecution and conviction for even the most egregious, reckless and criminal acts related to alcohol abuse.' The first suit sought $200 million in damages on behalf of Maria Pena, the mother of Maria Herrera and Dilcia Pena, and the grandmother of Herrera's two children. The second suit, filed on Thursday 15 August, sought $100 million on behalf of Maria Herrera's husband, Victor Herrera.

After hearing the many stories of police misbehaviour and corruption that came out at the trial, the District Attorney launched an official investigation into police misconduct in the 72nd Precinct. 'It was just an atmosphere that anything went. They just didn't care about the rules, thought that they were above the rules and they didn't apply to them,' said Derek Sills, a lawyer for the family.

On Third Avenue, at the site of the accident, a makeshift memorial to the victims contains a placard bearing the message 'We Want Justice'.

Joe Gray and his drinking pals were certainly guilty of serious misconduct, but a lot of people believe he got something of a raw deal. The case became the focal point for activists determined to make a stand against racism and police brutality in the NYPD, and Gray subsequently became a scapegoat for anti-police sentiment in the immigrant community. Back at the 72nd Precinct, according to one officer, 'People just view it for what it is – a really bad accident.' But the contents of Joesph Gray's car, searched by police after the accident, tell a different story. The minivan was found to contain two empty cans of Budweiser, along with a Mothers Against Drunk Driving ribbon that Gray's wife had left in the car – possibly as a message to her hard-drinking husband.

Difficult as it may be for many people to believe, 4 August 2001 was not a particularly wild and boozy night at the 72nd Precinct, but simply business as usual.

INTERNET SOURCES
Matt McBean, www.courttv.com/trials/gray_joseph
www.courttv.com/trials/gray_joesph/civilsuit
www.courttv.com/trials/gray_joseph/chronology
www.courttv.com/trials/gray_joseph/backgrounder

8. MURDEROUS OBSESSION

KENT MCGOWEN
Mikita Brottman

Kent McGowen may not have been the worst cop in history, but he might well have been one of the most pathetic – a braggart, a liar and a gun-happy fool, whose rejection by an older woman led him to kill. What seems most remarkable about this case, however, is not that McGowen was found guilty of murder, but that he managed to stay on the force after being fired from three other police departments and accumulating a stack of negative letters of reference. One claimed McGowen 'showed a crusader arrogance', another that he 'had no business' in law enforcement; another that he should have 'no contact with the public'. And yet four separate police departments chose to hire him as a cop. How was he allowed to move from one department to another after consistently being fired for serious infractions of duty? Did nobody ever check his references? How did this killer cop so frequently manage to bury his past?

Joseph Kenton McGowen was born in Midland, Texas, on 3 April 1965 into a wealthy family. His father, Bill McGowen, was originally a consultant for various oil groups who split off and founded his own company, which prospered during the oil boom of the late 70s and early 80s. The McGowen family were born-again Christians, who believed in the laying on of hands, speaking in tongues and the literal interpretation of the Bible – their home was called the 'Deuteronomy 28 Ranch'. They idolised their son, Kent, who matured into a troubled teenager fascinated by guns, a controlling and manipulative young man who displayed no compunction about twisting the truth to fit his own purposes; a man drawn to violence, especially against women.

In 1982, much to his parents' disappointment, Kent McGowen dropped out of high school and enlisted in the US Air Force. During a break from training in 1983 he married his long-time girlfriend Michelle, with whom he had a turbulent, on-again off-again relationship. Over time, Kent and Michelle would have four children, each conceived during a reconciliation in their troubled and sometimes violent marriage. Just fourteen months after joining the Air Force, McGowen decided he didn't like the discipline demanded by the military, and began to consider his next move. He wanted to be a cop.

His initial application to the Houston Police Department was rejected, however – he confessed on a questionnaire to smoking marijuana and being racially prejudiced – and so in July 1984 he enrolled in the Criminal Justice Center at the University of Houston, a kind of adult education programme for would-be cops. That summer, he took courses in everything from firearms training to the use of a baton, and the following January he entered the ranks of licensed police officers as an unpaid volunteer. The following year, 1985, he reapplied to the Houston Police Department, and this time he was accepted as a cadet.

Finally, Kent McGowen had what he wanted: the badge, the power, and the gun.

Officer JK McGowen quickly began to gain a bad reputation in the Houston Police Department, becoming known as a braggart, a compulsive liar, and a man with a violent hatred of women, whom he usually referred to as 'bitches' or 'pussies'. His fellow officers recall him boasting about his father's money, about the high-speed chases and shoot-outs he'd been involved in, about the women he'd picked up who were impressed by his uniform and gun. He soon got into trouble with his superiors for ignoring their advice, treating civilians discourteously, making foolhardy arrests and basically taking the law into his own hands. 'McGowen wanted to cash in on the uniform, get himself some road runners, groupies,' said a fellow officer. 'The kind of women who are turned on by the uniform.' In 1988 he became involved with a female officer, Sara Williams, but the relationship quickly degenerated into an ongoing feud, and both complained to their superiors about one another's behaviour.

On 9 January 1989, McGowen 'resigned' from the HPD, after it became obvious he simply wasn't cut out to be a cop. He was unable to control himself on the force, unable to curb his natural tendencies towards violence and selfish arrogance. His exit report, written by his commanding officer, summed things up very well:

Performance poor with a lack of maturity. A general bad attitude toward the department . . . In the time I supervised the employee, I did not observe any significant strengths worth noting . . . He has poor relationships with supervisors, brought on by his lack of orientation toward authority. Though tolerated by some peers, he is not respected by others . . . The employee talked about leaving as long as I knew him . . . When he gave notice, his actions turned from disrespectful to mutinous . . . The employee apparently enjoyed the excitement of police work, but was an arrogant malingering malcontent when placed under any form of supervision . . . He was a disruptive influence among peers, often giving advice when not requested or warranted.

Yet even this was not enough to prevent McGowen from being re-employed as a cop.

On 12 May 1989, despite his terrible reference report, Kent McGowen was employed at the nearby Tomball Police Department as a reserve patrolman – a voluntary, unpaid position – on the drug taskforce. Very quickly, however, the arrogant ex-cop fell into the same patterns of behaviour that got him fired from the Houston Police Department – poor judgement, dubious motives, an inclination to exaggerate, dishonesty, violence and hostility to women. The drug taskforce was mainly involved in small-time deals – local teenage kids selling negligible quantities of grass or cocaine. But his supervising officer observed that Kent McGowen seemed to be living in a fantasy world, talking constantly about huge drug busts, Colombian cartels, stolen weapons and international connections. It was as though he was trying to live out an episode of *Miami Vice* or *LAPD*. After months of this kind of behaviour, McGowen filed a complaint, claiming that members of a Colombian drug cartel had threatened his life. Tired of McGowen's fantasies, his supervising officer dismissed him from the reserves. In the meantime, his reapplication to the Houston Police Department had also been rejected.

But there were plenty of other Police Departments to choose from.

In February 1990, Kent McGowen took another position as an unpaid deputy, this time in the offices of Precinct Four in northwest Houston. He was issued with a uniform, a badge and a weapon, and smoothly resumed his law enforcement career – at least, for a while. On 27 March, less than two months after he was hired, Kent McGowen's commission was terminated after he got into a drunken fight while on duty. His exit report, however, made no mention of this incident. On 4 October of the same year, the 25-year-old Joseph Kent McGowen signed a tentative employment agreement, joining his fourth law employment agency in as many years, the Harris County Sheriff's Department. After short fire and safety courses, and a class in basic jail procedures, he was assigned to work at the county's jail in Franklin.

But McGowen was soon bored by working in the jail. There was very little action, few opportunities for him to engage in violent pursuits, to flash his badge and gun, to scare women. In May he applied yet again to be reinstated at the Houston Police Department, but his application was again rejected after he failed to meet the minimum psychological requirements after two separate evaluations. Instead, he applied to be transferred from the jail in Harris to a regular patrol job. And in April 1992, after nineteen months of working at the county jail, McGowen finally saw his coveted transfer come through. His new assignment was to patrol Olde Oaks, the forested, up-scale Houston suburb that was home to Susan White.

When Kent McGowen first met her, Susan White was an attractive 42-year-old blonde, a former nurse currently taking acting lessons and doing occasional work as a model. Her first marriage had ended in divorce, and her second husband had recently moved out of the family home, 3407 Amber Forest, where Susan continued to live with her seventeen-year-old son Jason. Things had rapidly gone downhill for Susan since her husband left. She was drinking too much and taking too many pills, and lived in constant fear of her home being repossessed, since her husband had stopped making mortgage payments. She had moved most of the furniture out of her home and into storage, in case it was claimed by creditors, and spent most of her time worrying about her son.

Ever since they had moved to Olde Oaks, Jason had been getting into all kinds of trouble. He'd been thrown out of school for pointing a BB gun at the bus driver, and was now in a 'special' school for troubled kids. He smoked and drank, and Susan suspected he sometimes did drugs as well. He had a string of young girlfriends, and when Susan was away, she often returned to neighbourhood complaints about wild parties going on at all hours of the night.

It remains unclear how Kent McGowen and Susan White first met, but it may have been after McGowen was called in to break up one of Jason's noisy parties. On the other hand, Susan White had a well-documented history of stopping deputies' cars as they circulated through Olde Oaks and readily calling officers for help, sometimes just to talk. She may well have done the same with McGowen. According to one of Susan's friends, McGowen had stopped Susan one day for speeding – she always drove as fast as possible – but instead of writing her a ticket, he'd asked her out. He said he'd noticed her before, coming and going through the neighbourhood, and found her very attractive. But Susan was out of his league; she was looking for a wealthy man to be her third husband. McGowen may have been attractive, in his cop's uniform with his dark hair and moustache, but he was too young for Susan, and she wasn't interested.

According to another of her friends, however, Susan confessed to having a one-night stand with the young cop, and then complained that he didn't seem to understand that she didn't want to see him any more. She claimed that McGowen was harassing her, and she was unhappy with his attention. She said that she'd refused to date him and he didn't like it; not only was he bothering her, but he also threatened to hurt Jason.

She said she had complained to the police department on more than one occasion, but they had done nothing about it.

What remains clear is that during late summer of 1992, Kent McGowen began hanging around Olde Oaks in the middle of the night, becoming increasingly obsessed with the glamorous single mother. He'd stop her repeatedly for speeding, come to her house to complain about Jason's music, and sometimes stop Jason and search his car for drugs. 'He comes to the house at night, but never when anyone's here,' Susan told a friend. 'He seems to know when I'm alone. I've stopped wearing little nighties to bed, just in case he knocks on the door after I've gone to sleep. I've been sleeping in old flannel gowns and big shirts.' She mentioned McGowen's creepy behaviour to a number of her friends, including her boyfriend Ray, but nobody seemed to take her very seriously. Susan was an actress, after all, with a penchant for melodrama.

In early August 1992, Kent McGowen stopped a teenaged boy named Mike Shaffer, a close friend of Jason's, and found him to be in possession of a small amount of marijuana. Instead of arresting him, however, McGowen promised Shaffer immunity from prosecution if he agreed to take part in a sting, buying a stolen gun from Jason with money McGowen promised him. Mike Shaffer agreed, and the sting went ahead. It seems fairly obvious that McGowen's main intention was to arrest Jason in order to get back at Susan White, or to further inveigle himself into her life, since these were teenaged kids, not dangerous gun-runners, and hardly involved in the kind of large-scale crime that necessitated a police sting.

On Saturday 22 August, at Mike Shaffer's request, Jason bought a stolen gun from a friend for $200, then met Mike in a parking lot at 11.30 at night. Officer Kent McGowen, in hiding nearby, watched Jason walk across the parking lot. In Shaffer's car, the two boys talked, then Jason pulled the stolen gun out of his pocket and handed it to Mike, who handed over the $200. As Jason walked back towards his car, McGowen barked an order into his radio, and three squad cars, sirens blazing, roared into the parking lot. A uniformed deputy jumped on top of Jason, pushed him to the ground and handcuffed his wrists behind his back. He was arrested and taken to jail, while Mike Shaffer was allowed to go free. It was pretty clear to Jason that the whole thing had been set up by McGowen.

When Susan White found out that the cop who'd been hassling her had got hold of her son, she was absolutely frantic. She was unable to get Jason out of jail until the following Monday, but she visited him and spoke to him on the phone, and Jason described everything that had happened. Susan was furious. She knew Jason was a troubled kid, but he definitely was not a gun-runner and he didn't deserve to be locked away in jail. As soon as she could, Susan White called Mike Shaffer and tried to get him to admit helping to set Jason up, but Mike was reluctant to talk. 'Don't you watch television, Mike?' Susan White asked angrily. 'Being an informant is a risky business. They get killed.' Next, she called Lieutenant Coons, Kent McGowen's boss, complaining about the sting and begging Coons to help her, telling him she was terrified of McGowen. She told him that she was convinced the gun deal was a set-up to get back at her, that McGowen had been hanging around her house at night and sexually harassing her, and that he'd threatened to hurt her son.

When McGowen arrived on duty at the police station that night, Lieutenant Coons informed him that Susan

White had levelled serious charges against him, including accusations of sexual harassment and making threats about what he'd do to her if she wouldn't date him. The arrogant cop denied that he even knew the woman, dismissing her allegations as the rantings of an over-protective mother anxious about her son. McGowen added that Mike Shaffer had told him how Susan had called him over the weekend and made a comment about informants getting killed, maintaining that this constituted a threat on Mike Shaffer's life, and requesting a warrant for Susan White's arrest under the charge of 'retaliation'. When Coons agreed, McGowen added that he'd be happy to serve the warrant himself. Meanwhile, Jason was released on bail and returned home to his mother's house in Olde Oaks.

At about midnight the following Monday, 25 August 1992, Officer Kent McGowen and two other deputies arrived at 3407 Amber Forest to serve Susan White with an arrest warrant on the charge of retaliation. McGowen rang the doorbell, and Susan peered through the leaded glass panels of her front doors and asked who was there. When she realised it was Officer McGowen, the man who'd been harassing her for weeks, she went into a panic and refused to open the door. Instead, she grabbed the telephone, ran upstairs, dialled 911 and told them that she needed help immediately. She told the operator that Kent McGowen had made sexual advances towards her in the past and had threatened her son, and she was terrified to open the door. 'This is a deputy who thinks he rules the world,' she said. 'McGowen has made sexual advances toward me.'

Susan White begged the operator to send somebody else over to the house, then began shouting at the officers out of her bedroom window. 'Get McGowen away from my house,' she shouted. 'I want him out of my yard and off my property ... You don't go peeking in ladies' bedroom windows.' The operator promised that more police were on the way, and Susan shouted to the officers that she'd come out quietly on the condition that McGowen left the premises. Ignoring her pleas, Officer McGowen instructed his deputies to break down the front door.

He'd waited a long time for this, and he wasn't going to let anything get in his way.

As the three cops started beating down Susan White's front door, she continued to beg for help on the telephone. 'They're trying to break into my house,' she pleaded. 'They say they're detectives but I've been threatened by one of them ... They're breaking my door down.' At that point, the front door broke down, setting off the burglar alarm. Susan White began to scream in terror, and she moved towards the gun she kept in the drawer of her bedside table.

Kent McGowen charged into the house, pulled out his gun and ran straight up the stairs to Susan's bedroom. The two deputies stayed behind, searching the down-stairs rooms as they'd been taught to do, but McGowen made a beeline for the master bedroom, as though he'd been there before. Jason – the alleged 'gun-runner' – remained in his bedroom, quivering with fear.

'Drop the gun,' the two deputies heard McGowen shout over the wail of the burglar alarm. 'Drop the gun, I said. Drop the gun.' The next thing they heard was the sound of three shots, as Officer McGowen shot Susan White through the face, chest and right arm.

His warrant had been served.

At first, Kent McGowen assumed he would get away with the murder of Susan White, just as he had got away with so many of the other crimes he'd committed in the past. He strutted arrogantly around the police station, boasting about how he'd shot Susan White in the face, about how he'd 'shot to kill'. He got hold of a copy of the 911 tape and played it for the other cops to listen to; he even boasted about how he was planning to get hold of the shell casings from his bullets to keep as a souvenir of his killing. As soon as the case was investigated, however, it was obvious that nothing seemed to fit. Why had it been necessary to serve the warrant in the middle of the night? Why was this woman with a clean police record considered so dangerous? Why didn't McGowen check the rooms downstairs before storming into Susan's bedroom? How did he know where her bedroom was? Even more disturbing, why was McGowen's first shot directed at her head, and not her body or extremities, as he'd been taught? Since Susan White was left handed, she couldn't have been pointing a gun at him, as he'd claimed.

The conclusion seemed obvious: Kent McGowen's claim of self-defence was a lie.

The case went to trial, but here, as elsewhere, McGowen seemed to have the uncanny capacity of managing to slip through the net. In 1994, a Houston jury convicted Joseph Kent McGowen of murder and sentenced him to fifteen years in prison. However, according to Texas law at the time, anyone sentenced to fifteen years or less was eligible to remain free on bail while the conviction was appealed – a statute that has since been revised. McGowen's wealthy family had no problem coming up with his $10,000 bail money, and Kent McGowen was released while his defence team worked on his appeal.

It took another three years for the appeal to be heard and then, to many people's surprise, it was a success. In 1997, a Texas appellate court ordered a new trial for

McGowen, ruling that the 1994 trial judge made a mistake in not allowing defence attorneys to make an opening statement before they began presenting their witnesses to the jury. The confusion over the right of the defence to make an opening statement came after the prosecution decided not to make such a statement. The court declared a mistrial.

In 1997, the family of Susan White won a $5.3 million federal judgement against Harris County, which was responsible for hiring Kent McGowen despite his many negative references, but when the original trial was overturned, the federal judgement was overturned as well, and Harris County was dismissed as a defendant. This meant that Susan's family would never get their compensation. Susan White's mother said the decision to relieve the sheriff's department of liability was disappointing. 'We feel like Harris County helped him pull the trigger,' she said. 'It's not the money, it's the idea of how he could get that arrest warrant.'

It was almost ten years before justice was done in the case of Kent McGowen. For ten years, he'd been living comfortably, supported by his parents. The case didn't return to trial until 28 March 2002, when the jury came back from the Easter break to decide that McGowen should serve twenty years behind bars, leaving him ineligible to remain free on bail while appealing the conviction. Susan White's mother expressed her relief at the court's decision. 'It's been some tough years, but our family will get some relief now that he's in prison,' she said. 'He should have gotten death. But we feel better to have him in prison, where he can't kill again.'

It took Kent McGowen ten years to be brought to trial – a shocking length of time. What remains even more shocking, however, is how the crime could have been allowed to happen in the first place. Everybody knows there are plenty of bad cops around, but for a cop to be fired from three different police departments, condemned as aggressive and dangerous, and *still* re-hired as a police officer raises some very serious questions about law enforcement practices in Texas.

BIBLIOGRAPHY

Casey, Kathryn, *A Warrant to Kill*, Avon Books: NY, 2002.

Minton, James, 'Baker couple relieved killer of daughter ordered to prison,' *Baker Advocate*, 16 April 2002, 10.

9. MURDER FRENZY

GJ SCHAEFER: THE COP TURNED SERIAL KILLER
Mikita Brottman

Bad cops are hardly rare, but it seems difficult to imagine a worse case than that of Gerard John Schaefer, convicted of two murders and suspected of involvement in at least eleven more. Although he wasn't a cop for long, it seems likely that Schaefer joined the police force with the express purpose of using his police privileges to abduct and murder unsuspecting young girls. Killer cops are not uncommon, but for someone to become a policeman for the express purpose of killing must be rather unusual. But then, everything about GJ Schaefer was unusual, including the fact that his first murder probably took place when he was only 22 years old.

Gerard John Schaefer was born on 25 March 1946 in Wisconsin, the first of three children. His father was a travelling salesman for Kimberly Clark, and not long after Gerard's birth the family moved to an affluent suburb of Atlanta, Georgia, where Schaefer did well at a Catholic parochial school. His relationship with his parents was constantly tense and turbulent. He recalls his father as being 'always critical,' and his mother being 'always on my back to do better'. Schaefer seems to have been a troubled child. He recalled 'discovering' women's panties at the age of twelve, which is when he first started to masturbate while wearing them. He also confessed to practising masochistic bondage as a young child, and fantasising to images of sexual violence. 'I would fantasise about hurting other people,' he later confessed, 'women in particular.' Like many serial killers, he was preoccupied with death even as a young child, and recalls sometimes reaching the point where he 'didn't know what was fact and what was fantasy'.

In 1960, the well-to-do Schaefer family moved to Fort Lauderdale, Florida, where they promptly joined the local yacht and country clubs. Four years later, the eighteen-year-old Gerard Schaefer met an attractive seventeen-year-old girl named Sandy Steward at a high school dance, and the two soon began dating. Sandy Steward later described her new boyfriend as a 'dazzling young stranger' who swept her off her feet, impressing both herself and her family with his impeccable manners; she considered him 'gentle and sweet, bright and polite,' and 'unfailingly eager to please'. Sandy spent much of her time with Schaefer for the next couple of years, and found him unfailingly gentle and considerate as a lover.

Despite his affair with Sandy, Schaefer applied to join the priesthood in 1964, but was promptly rejected. Instead, he enrolled in Broward County Community College, where he reportedly turned in a mediocre academic performance. Meanwhile, Sandy Steward quickly began to realise that her wonderful new boyfriend wasn't quite the person he appeared to be. He seemed increasingly beset by doubts and personal anxieties, and when their relationship began to lose its momentum, she broke up with him, no longer wanting to function as his therapist. Schaefer took the break-up badly, stalking his ex-girlfriend for a while and sending her a series of melodramatic letters and poems.

In 1967, Gerard Schaefer graduated from Broward Community College with an associate degree in business administration and entered Florida Atlantic University in Boca Raton, hoping to certify as a high school teacher. He managed to avoid the draft after failing a number of psychological tests (and confessing to wearing women's underwear), and in December 1968 – five months after his own parents had filed for divorce – he married his new girlfriend, Martha Fogg. As part of his teaching certification, Schaefer was assigned as a student teacher in a local high school, but he soon ran into trouble and the Principal removed him a few weeks later, citing his 'totally inappropriate behavior'. He was moved on to another school but quickly lost his position there as well. Finally he dropped out of university altogether, citing 'marital difficulties' as the reason.

But Gerard Schaefer's marriage was the least of his problems.

His first murder appears to have taken place in September 1969, when he was 22 years old and a student at Florida Atlantic University. On 8 September, a former neighbour of his – a girl named Leigh Hainline Bonadies, who Schaefer claimed used to undress provocatively in front of her bedroom window – disappeared from her home; her husband discovered a note pinned to their apartment door saying that Leigh was going away to Miami. He recalled a suspicious story his wife had recently told him about an old friend of hers, a guy who'd lived three doors down, who had recently been offering her large sums of money to do some 'undercover work' for the CIA. This neighbour turned out to be Schaefer, who admitted that he had been talking to Leigh on the phone and had agreed to give her a ride to the airport that morning, but she never showed up. When Schaefer was arrested for murder four years later, a search of his belongings stored at his mother's house turned up several pieces of Leigh's jewellery, including a locket inscribed with her name.

Three months after Leigh Hainline Bonadies disappeared, Gerard Schaefer appears to have struck again.

On 18 December 1969, an attractive cocktail waitress named Carmen Hallock had lunch with a friend at the Coral Ridge Shopping Center in Fort Lauderdale. Carmen told her friend that she had an appointment at five o'clock that day with a teacher from the junior college, who'd told her that he wanted to employ her to do some kind of undercover work for the government. She said he'd offered her a good salary, plus her own apartment in New York or Washington D.C. No trace was ever found of Carmen Hallock until Schaefer's belongings were searched in 1973, when two of her gold teeth and her shamrock pin were found in his collections of murderous souvenirs.

In 1970, two young girls – nine-year-old Peggy Rahn and eight-year-old Wendy Stevenson – disappeared from Pompano Beach after last being spotted with a white man in his twenties, matching Schaefer's description, who was spotted buying them ice-cream. The girls were never found and Schaefer was never charged, though prosecutors publicly accused him of the crime. Later, in a letter from prison, he wrote 'Peggy and Wendy just happened to come along at a time when I was curious . . . I found both of them very satisfactory.'

In the same year, Schaefer returned to Florida Atlantic University in an attempt to complete his degree, and in the same year his wife Martha filed for divorce, citing her husband's 'extreme cruelty' as the reason. By October, when the divorce became final, Schaefer was already involved with another woman, a young secretary named Teresa Dean. The two married soon after Schaefer's university graduation in 1971, when he was finally awarded a degree in geography. His failed internship meant that Schaefer's teaching certificate was never granted but, by this time, he had a new career path in mind.

After failing as a priest and a teacher, GJ Schaefer had come to the realisation that he was perfectly cut out to be a cop.

It seemed the ideal vocation for the brutish young man. He had a long-standing obsession with guns and violence, loved to assert his authority over others, especially women, and had always enjoyed hunting down animals in the swamps. Schaefer seems to have regarded the police uniform and accoutrements as remarkably useful tools for winning the trust and confidence of vulnerable young girls. First, however, he needed to be accepted by a police department. An application to the Broward County Sheriff's Office was turned down after Schaefer failed a mandatory psychological test, but in 1970, he was hired by the Wilton Manors Police Department. He was sent back to Broward Community College to attend Police Academy, from which he graduated in December 1971, when he first hit the streets to begin his six-month probationary term.

A short time later, another young woman disappeared.

On 5 January 1972, a man named William Hutchens went to the Fort Lauderdale police and reported that his wife Belinda had gone missing after he'd spotted her getting into a stranger's blue Datsun – the same kind of car that Schaefer drove. Belinda Hutchens's body was never discovered. However, after Schaefer's arrest six months later, investigators found a little black book among his property, listing William Hutchens's name and phone number. Days later, Hutchens, who had never met Schaefer, identified the killer cop's blue Datsun as the car that took away his wife on her last ride.

There seems little doubt that GJ Schaefer was responsible for the murder and abduction of Leigh Hainline

Bonadies, Carmen Hallock and Belinda Hutchens. Personal items belonging to each of these three women were discovered among Schaefer's 'treasure chest' after his arrest. However, since none of their bodies have ever been found, and since there hasn't been sufficient evidence to link Schaeffer to their disappearances, no charges against him have ever been brought in these cases.

As a police officer, Gerard Schaefer quickly turned out to be 'badge happy', allegedly obsessed with writing traffic tickets and stopping attractive young women and asking them for dates. He was unpopular on the force, and his foolhardy and inappropriate behaviour soon got him into trouble with his superiors. In April 1972, he was fired from Wilton Manors Police Department for his 'poor judgment' and a series of 'dumb mistakes'. His former boss, Captain Scott, refused to write him a letter of recommendation and, as a result, he was turned down by all the other police departments he applied to. Finally, Schaefer took the situation into his own hands and forged himself a glowing letter of recommendation from Captain Scott; in June, he was finally accepted into the Martin County Police Department. His reference letter was never checked out.

In July 1972, just 22 days after starting back on the streets as a cop, GJ Schaefer was cruising along a quiet freeway in Stuart, Florida, when he came across two teenaged hitch-hikers, Nancy Trotter and Pamela Sue Wells. After reprimanding the girls for hitch-hiking, which he dishonestly told them was against the law in Florida, he drove them back to the halfway house where they were staying and offered to give them a ride to the beach the following day. The two girls agreed, trusting Schaefer as a uniformed officer of the law. The next day, he picked them up as promised, but instead of driving the girls to the beach, he drove them to a heavily wooded area about eight miles south of Blind Creek in St Lucie County.

Here, after pulling his gun on the girls, the degenerate cop gagged and handcuffed them, put nooses round their necks, balanced them both on tree stumps so they'd hang themselves if they lost their balance, then left the area for a few moments, promising to return. While he was gone, however, Nancy and Pamela managed to wriggle out of their nooses and handcuffs and they fled to the nearest police station. Schaefer, knowing there was no way out, confessed to the crime, saying that he'd picked up the girls while they were hitch-hiking and simply intended to 'give them a good scare', to teach them to be more responsible in the future. But his boss didn't buy it. Gerard Schaefer was arrested, immediately dismissed from the Sheriff's office, convicted of assault, and sentenced in December 1972 to a year in jail for kidnapping, plus three years probation.

Still, with time off for good behaviour, he could easily have been out of jail in six months.

Schaefer's sentence, however, did not begin until January of the following year and, not one to waste any time, the cut-throat cop made the most of his last few weeks of freedom. At this stage in his murderous career, Schaefer seems to have become obsessed with abducting and murdering girls in pairs. He later wrote:

> Doing doubles is far more difficult than doing singles, but on the other hand it also puts one in a position to have twice as much fun. There can be some lively discussions about which of the victims will get to be killed first. When you have a pair of teenaged bimbolinas bound hand and foot and ready for a

session with the skinning knife, neither one of the little devils wants to be the one to go first. And they don't mind telling you quickly why their best friend should be the one to die.

On 27 September 1972, two teenaged girls, seventeen-year-old Susan Place and sixteen-year-old Georgia Jessup, disappeared from Susan's home in Oakland Park, Fort Lauderdale. Susan's mother told police that the girls were last seen with a suspicious-looking man calling himself 'Jerry Shepherd', who was supposed to be taking them to the beach 'to play guitar'. Dubious of the tall stranger, Mrs Place jotted down his licence plate number as the girls got into his car – although, unfortunately, she misread one of the digits. Less than four weeks later, on 23 October, fourteen-year-olds Mary Alice Briscolina and Elsie Lina Farmer were added to the missing list. Items of their jewellery were eventually found among Schaefer's belongings.

On 8 January 1973, nineteen-year-old Iowa residents Collette Goodenough and Barbara Ann Wilcox left home in order to hitch-hike to Florida. No trace of either girl was found until April, when, in what was becoming a frightening pattern, some of their personal belongings were found among Schaefer's stash, including a book of poetry, Barbara's driving licence and Collette's passport. Skeletal remains of both victims were later found at Port Saint Lucie – the same wooded, swampy area where Schaefer had taken Nancy Trotter and Pamela Sue Wells – but no cause of death could be found, and no charges were ever filed against him. Schaefer began serving his one-year sentence for abduction on 15 January 1973.

In March of that same year, bones and teeth belonging to Georgia Jessup and Susan Place were discovered in Blind Creek, near Hutchinson Island, and the girls were identified from their dental records. When Schaefer's licence plate turned out to be very similar to that jotted down by Mrs Place after seeing the girls drive off with the suspicious-looking 'Jerry Shepherd', there was finally enough evidence to convict this brutal officer of murder. On 27 September 1973, Gerard John Schaefer was convicted of the killing of Susan Place and Georgia Jessup, and received two concurrent life sentences.

Schaefer's 21-year-old wife Teresa visited him only once in prison, and that was to present him with divorce papers. As soon as the divorce came through, she promptly married Schaefer's public defender, 45-year-old Elton Schwartz. Much later, in September 1990, Schaefer decided to ask the court for a retrial based on this apparent conflict of interest, writing 'Elton Schwartz had a motive for all this. My young wife, who was smitten by his attentions. Sex with a young girl. It's an ancient motive.' This appeal, like many others, was thrown out of court.

Among Schaefer's 'treasure trove' of murderous mementos discovered when his mother's home was searched in April 1973 were approximately fifty pages of writing and illustrations detailing a series of narratives of sadistic murder. The lascivious lawman contended that these writings and drawings were pure fantasy, and although this hoard of 'killer fiction' was confiscated by investigators, Schaefer continued writing violent stories from his jail cell. The rest of his time was spent filing nineteen appeals against his sentence, each of which was summarily dismissed by an increasingly weary judge. In 1979 he declared himself 'married' to a Filipina 'mail order bride' who moved in with his father, and with whom he was permitted to enjoy conjugal visits until she obtained a green card and disappeared. In September 1985 Schaefer was accused of planning to escape from jail, and packed off to Starke Prison, home of Florida's death row.

Here, his new pals included serial killers Ted Bundy and Ottis Toole, both of whom – he claims – looked up to him like a criminal mentor. According to Schaefer, 'Bundy was always 100% respectful of me. I treated him as a supplicant, while others were hanging on every word.' Bundy allegedly confessed that he'd been inspired by Schaefer to kill two victims on a single day in 1974, or to 'do a double,' as Schaefer might have put it. With other prisoners, Schaefer acted as a jailhouse 'lawyer,' writing briefs for fellow cons then promptly selling them out to the authorities in the hope of getting his own sentence reduced. Not surprisingly, he quickly began to gain a reputation as a rat and a snitch.

And then in February 1989, in his maximum security cell in Starke Prison, Schaefer's life suddenly changed when he was visited by a fond memory from the past. He received a letter from his former high school girlfriend Sandy Steward, now known as Sondra London, a single mother working as a technical writer but interested in expanding her literary horizons. London had recently read *The Stranger Beside Me*, Ann Rule's book about her youthful relationship with serial killer Ted Bundy, and decided she had a great story of her own to tell. After all, she too had her very own ex-boyfriend-turned-serial killer, murderous cop Gerard Schaefer. The collaboration between Schaefer and London lasted from 1989 until 1992, during which time Sondra made a series of visits to her ex-boyfriend in Starke Prison. According to London, although Schaefer liked to characterise himself as 'a former street cop who is in open population in perhaps America's most repressive hellhole,' she describes him as 'a nebbish:

portly, pale, balding, and half-blind ... like a middle-aged, deskbound clerk gone to seed.' This new Gerard Schaefer was a far cry from the handsome stranger who swept her off her feet at the high school dance in 1964.

Between March and July of 1989, Schaefer sent London a series of stories in three sections, entitled 'Whores', 'Starke Stories' and 'Actual Fantasies'. This last section included many of the stories and drawings used as evidence in his 1973 murder trial. A limited edition of the volume comprising these three sections was copyrighted and published in 1989 by Media Queen Ltd, Sondra London's publishing company. After *Killer Fiction* was finalised, another batch of stories was published as *Beyond Killer Fiction*, including narratives with such graphic titles as 'Blonde on a Stick', 'Flies in her Eyes', 'Murder Frenzy' and 'Gator Bait'. Fairly typical of Schaefer's style – which seems to have been heavily influenced by Harry Crews, who taught the creative writing classes Schaefer took at Florida Atlantic University – is this passage from a story called 'Powerline Road':

> *The last I checked she had rotted away to nothing but her torso from her waist to the remnants of her backside. Oddly enough when her body swelled up during decomposition the gas must have pushed a load of shit down into her rectum, because when I examined her hole with a stick it came out all shitty.*
>
> *She's still there now in her unmarked grave and sometimes I feel sorry not so much for her as her family because it seems they must have really cared about her. She was a whore and a tease who was no good and I'm sorry too that I didn't spend more time enjoying her body when I had the chance, rather than just dumping it in a hole before it even became stiff.*

This was the first one and they say the first one is the hardest. So far though the first has been the best body-wise. I think there will surely be others.

Schaefer's relationship with Sondra London fell apart when he began to tell her details of his various crimes, along with threats about what he would have done to her were she ever to reveal them to the police. When Sondra arranged for a television interview, which Schaefer interpreted as 'selling him out', he threatened to call on his alleged connections with biker gangs, white supremacists and Satanists to have London and her daughter abducted, raped and murdered. She quickly broke off her collaboration with the vicious ex-cop and asked the prison to forbid him to write to her any more. Unable to accept defeat, Schaefer then embarked on a campaign of revenge by filing a series of lawsuits against London and various other crime writers who, he claimed, had libelled him by tagging him as a 'serial killer'. The cases were all thrown out of court when the judge ruled that Schaefer was quite clearly 'a serial killer undoubtedly linked to numerous murders' and therefore 'libel-proof under the law'.

It must have been especially maddening, however, when Schaefer discovered that his former girlfriend Sondra London had jilted him yet again – and this time for his prison-mate in Starke, a younger and more attractive serial killer by the name of Danny Rolling. In 1993, Sondra London received an ominous valentine from Schaefer. 'Hello Whore,' it began.

The word on the yard is that the queen of the sluts is romancing Danny Rolling . . . I was so right about you, Sondra: Whore. Pure fucking whore. A whore and a rat . . . Valentine, you're mine. Why you out front licking

Rolling's ego? I know what you're up to: money. You're gonna get Danny Boy fried while you make a buck off his misery. Right? . . . Should I see my name involved in any of this Rollings crap you're at the center of then I'm going to put you and your whoredaughter on my list of unfinished business . . .

On the morning of 3 December 1995, Gerard John Schaefer was found by prison guards, stabbed to death in his cell at Starke Prison. His blood-drenched body had sustained over forty wounds, predominantly about the head and neck. Two months later, prison officials filed a murder charge against 33-year-old Vincent Rivera, who claims to have quarrelled with Schaefer after he took the last cup of water from a dispenser on their cell block. Rivera was indicted for Schaefer's murder on 1 February 1996, but he claims he is innocent and has been framed for murder by the prison inspector who headed the investigation. Police still suspect Schaefer of the murders of at least eleven other women and girls, apart from the two he was convicted of killing, and his many petitions and appeals were repeatedly denied.

Whether Schaefer's death was part of a cover-up or just another cold-blooded prison murder, the execution of this killer cop was clearly long overdue.

BIBLIOGRAPHY

Dorschner, John, 'The Devil's Triangle,' *Tropic*, 30 January 1994, pp. 7–13, 18–21.

King, Brian, ed., *Lustmord: The Writings and Artefacts of Murderers*, Burbank, CA: Bloat Books, 1996.

Schaefer, GJ and Sondra London, *Killer Fiction*, Venice, CA: Feral House, 1995.

Walsh, John, *Tears of Rage*, New York: Pocket Books, 1997.

10. BLACK MOTHER

BAD COPS, BIOLOGY AND THE HINDU DEATH GODDESS
Simon Whitechapel

If human consciousness didn't crawl glacially by in seconds and minutes, the paradox is that it would be much more fun to watch glaciers. If we perceived in centuries and millennia instead, glaciers would lash out and back from mountains like great white whips. If we could perceive in periods even longer than millennia, we could watch mountains rise and fall too and observe the effects of the greatest crash in history: the collision of a raft weighing trillions of tonnes with the underbelly of the world's largest continent.

The continent is Asia and the raft is India. Millions of years ago it was a gigantic island off the coast of Australia, lying south of the equator and separated from Asia by the sea of Tethys. Travelling northward at an estimated rate of ten metres a century it collided with Asia about 45 million years ago and, if that was an example of an irresistible force meeting an immovable object, the result has been the Himalayas, the kilometre-high rumples in a carpet of solid rock. In Sanskrit, the ancient language of northern India, *Himalaya* means 'Ice-Home', but they're not only the home of *hima*, 'ice', they're also the home of Shiva, the Hindu god of death, destruction, and rebirth. Shiva has a more famous wife, Kali, the goddess of death, destruction and rebirth and one legend of her tells that Shiva once chopped her corpse into fifty-three pieces and scattered them over the earth. Her *yoni* – her cunt – fell to earth as a great stone in the Himalayas at Guwahati in Assam, where her priests now celebrate its presence with the mass-sacrifice of sheep and doves.[1]

Gentle vegetarian Hinduism has its dark side, you see, and Kali is the dark heart of its dark side: call upon her as *Kaalii Māā*, 'Mother Kali', and you are calling on the 'Black Mother', because Kali means 'black' – the black of old, dried blood. But Kali herself is blue – the blue of an Indian corpse three days dead, in summer heat. In traditional representations of her she wears a garland of skulls around her neck, clutching a severed male head in one of her ten hands. Blood is gushing from the head into a bowl held by another of her ten hands and Shiva lies beneath her feet: she is trampling on him, making it easy to see her as a champion of the oppressed, weak female overturning strong male, victim turned victimiser. I like to see her like that myself, but if patriotism is the last refuge of a scoundrel, religion has always been one of the first, and maybe Kali laughs at the abuse of authority in modern India rather than shouts with rage. English has borrowed many words from Indian languages, but one of the most common helps show whose side Kali might really be on. 'Thug' is a Hindi word once applied to followers of Kali who worshipped her with murder and theft.[2] Maybe you could call them Kali's pubic lice: India is shaped like a triangle and could be called *kali ki yoni*, Kali's cunt, gripped in an endless orgasm of pain and degradation.

The *thugs* were suppressed by the British Raj,[3] but their worship of Kali carried on in other ways: George Orwell (1903–50) described his memories of the Indian Imperial Police, for which he worked in Burma, as 'wretched prisoners squatting in the reeking cages of the lock-ups, the grey cowed faces of the long-term convicts, the scarred buttocks of the men who had been flogged with bamboos, the women and children howling when their menfolk were led away under arrest'.[4] We should note that Orwell adds 'our criminal law' in India was 'far more humane than in England', but native Indian justice would probably not have been any gentler and might have been much harsher. Nevertheless, the indigenous Indian middle-class resented the fact that foreigners were mistreating their lower classes and campaigned for independence and, just as some Irish nationalists – and some Jewish ones – supported Hitler during the Second World War,[5] so some Indian nationalists supported the Japanese. The Japanese, who treated Asian prisoners even worse than European ones during the Second World War, would have been worse overlords, but the British were definitely bad: some historians claim that the Raj allowed millions to die in famines rather than break the rules of free trade and that the Bengali famine during the Second World War, which again may have killed millions, was engineered by politicians such as Winston Churchill to divert food to the British Isles.[6]

When the Indian nationalists won their fight against such exploitation and India became independent in 1947, the country was, like Gaul, divided into three parts: one retained the name of India and had a Hindu majority; the other two, separated by the new India but intended as a single state, were called East and West Pakistan and had Muslim majorities. This partition of British India involved the migration of millions of people and resulted in hundreds of thousands of deaths in massacre and counter-massacre. East and West Pakistan – the name literally means 'land of the pure'[7] – became separate states in 1971 after the people of East Pakistan voted for independence. The military dictatorship of West Pakistan responded by fighting a civil war in which its troops were responsible for the mass murder of Bengali men and the mass rape of Bengali women. When India intervened to drive West Pakistani troops out, Indian troops carried on the massacres and rapes, and some estimates of the final number of dead go above one million.[8]

This very brutal, very recent shared history may be part of the explanation for the brutality and corruption of police in these three countries. West Pakistan is now known simply as Pakistan, East Pakistan as Bangladesh, 'land of the Bengalis', and both, like the India that separates them, are still very poor. The tradition of oppression established, or rather continued, under the British Raj can therefore still flourish, because there are still huge numbers of very poor people to practise it on. For example, child beggars and child labourers, or even child slaves, are common on the subcontinent (as India, Pakistan, and Bangladesh are collectively known), and the police take advantage of that by harassing and extorting money out of children living on the streets. But they sometimes go even further. In the West the police, in their official capacity, generally try to catch paedophiles; on the subcontinent the police, in their official capacity, often are paedophiles, arresting street-children in order to sexually abuse them. One infamous case that came to international attention in 1993 was that of a thirteen-year-old boy called Mohammad Shawkat, who was raped by two policemen in the Bangladeshi capital Dhaka. He went to the Dhaka Medical College Hospital to be treated for rectal injuries, where he made the possibly fatal mistake of describing how he had acquired them. Newspapers in Dhaka repeated his allegations and the two policemen were suspended, although there is no record that charges were ever brought against them. That would perhaps have been difficult, because the complainant disappeared from hospital shortly after making his complaint. One version of the story says that he went into hiding for fear of retribution by the police, another that his disappearance was in itself retribution by the police, namely, that the police had kidnapped and murdered him.

Two years later, in 1995, another case came to international attention in which the Bangladeshi police had apparently tried to learn from their mistake with Mohammad Shawkat: this time they didn't allow their victim to stay alive to complain about them. In the north-western town of Dinajpur, near the Indian border, a fourteen-year-old girl called Yasmin Akhter was given a lift home to her mother in a police van. She probably didn't want the lift, because she was later found dead on the roadside. The police claimed that she had been killed when she jumped from the van while it was moving, but that was an excuse that inculpated the officers: why had she wanted to jump from the van? Her death was probably the only unusual thing about the case: in the West there were once complaints about the way women alleging rape were treated unsympathetically by the police; on the subcontinent, the police treat women alleging rape unsympathetically to the extent of raping them again. At other times, they carry out rapes in ways like the one already described: by tricking or forcing women into police vehicles or police stations.

A song by the American punk band the Dead Kennedys called *Police Truck* (1980) shows that subcontinental police are by no means unique in this – one line goes 'There's six of us, babe, so suck on my dick' – but the rape and murder of fourteen-year-old girls are not something the American police would think they could easily get away with. If the Bangladeshi police thought they could easily get away with the rape and murder of Yasmin Akhter, they were wrong: after they tried to cover the crime up, there were public protests and an official inquiry and though its results were never made public[9] the three accused policemen were nevertheless found guilty and imprisoned in 1997.[10] However, prison may simply have offered them further opportunities for the sexual abuse of children: one of the chronic scandals of subcontinental justice is the imprisoning of children on trumped-up charges in adult prisons, where they provide services like cleaning and sex to the adult prisoners. In Western eyes, this kind of thing is like Sadean satire come to life, but we should remember that Sadean satire, at the time de Sade was writing it, was actually based on life: children were abused in similar ways in eighteenth- and nineteenth-century Europe. Perhaps this was because eighteenth- and nineteenth-century Europe was like twentieth- and twenty-first-century India, Pakistan, and Bangladesh: very many people had barely enough to survive and there was enormous overcrowding in the cities.

The film *Snuff* (1976) was advertised with the line 'The film that could only be made in South America . . . where Life is CHEAP!', but that's obviously untrue. Genuine snuff movies could be, and perhaps have been, made in many other parts of the world, because life is cheap in many other parts of the world where over-population meets extreme poverty. De Sade examined the phenomenon in his book *Juliette* (1798):

An important question arises here: its resolution will not, it seems to me, be beneath the attention of literary folk, and we put it to them with hopes of having it resolved by them. Does the corruption of manners, in a race, come from the weakness of its government, from its location, or from overcrowding in its great cities? Despite what is established here, Juliette, it is not from location that moral corruption arises, for there is as

*much moral disorder in the northern cities of London
and Paris as in the southern cities of Messina and
Naples; and it is not on the weakness of a government,
for the government is, in these matters, much more
severe in the north than in the south, and corruption is
nevertheless the same. The corruption of manners,
whatever the climate or government may be, comes from
nothing but an excessive crowding together of individuals
in the same place: whatever becomes crowded becomes
corrupt, and every government that wishes to avoid such
corruption must fight over-population and, above all, set
up organisations to promote chastity.*

A sane human being does not harm people whose
welfare his own welfare depends on, but when there are
very large numbers of people in a single place, his
welfare depends on very few of them and he can, given
the opportunity, harm the others with impunity. Many
of those who go into organisations like the police are
undoubtedly seeking such opportunities: policing is an
authoritarian profession attracting authoritarian personalities, and sadism is based on the exercising of
authority. The subcontinent, however, and particularly
that part of it known as India, offers particular opportunities to the authoritarian sadist, because not only is
there a ready supply of victims in India, there is also a
ready supply of excuses for victimising them. The
fissures of recent history are still open and bleeding in
India, most notoriously in Kashmir, which was divided
between India and Pakistan in 1947: Pakistan now has
a province called Azad Kashmir, or 'Free Kashmir', and
India has a state called Jammu and Kashmir and is
determined, despite the Muslim majority there, to hold
on to it, because the loss of Kashmir would undoubtedly
encourage secessionists in other parts of India.

India has accordingly adopted the tactic used by West Pakistan against the secessionists of East Pakistan: terror. The Indian policing of Kashmir has been extremely brutal, but the tortures employed by the police there and against secessionist movements in other states differ only in scale, not in kind, from those employed by the police in every state in India. When men do things a lot, they give nicknames to what they do, and so the Indian police have given nicknames to the tortures they carry out on prisoners:

The Aeroplane: *The prisoner's hands, or sometimes just his thumbs, are tied together behind his back and he is hoisted into the air so that his full weight hangs from his arms. The pain rapidly becomes excruciating and joints can be permanently dislocated or crippled.*

The Bombay Cuff: *A variant on the aeroplane in which the prisoner's hands are tied behind his back and he is left resting with his full weight on a pipe placed beneath his knees.*

The Roller: *The prisoner is held face-down while two policemen stand atop a wooden beam and roll it up and down his thighs and calves. The pain is again excruciating and there can be permanent and sometimes fatal sequelae: doctors working in the Kashmiri city Srinagar have recognised a special medical syndrome called 'physical torture nephropathy', which results from shredded muscle passing into the blood and damaging and sometimes destroying the kidneys.*

The Cog Needle: *A thin metal rod is passed through the navel or up the anus or through the soft tissue of the arms or legs.*

The Bellary: *A stick smeared with chilli paste is*

*pushed up the anus, causing severe prolonged
inflammation and pain.*[11]

The last torture, at least, dates back to the Raj and
before, as do the more usual beatings and deprivation
of food and water, but the Indian police have also
adopted modern techniques such as the use of electricity. Sexual abuse of male and female prisoners
is also common, and is used against the female relatives
of suspects or exiles. The north-western state of Punjab,
also split between India and Pakistan in 1947, has
a secessionist movement based, like the one in Kashmir,
on religion: militant Sikhs are trying to establish an
independent state called Khalistan (which, like Pakistan,
means 'Land of the Pure'). When the Golden Temple,
the central Sikh shrine at Amritsar, was occupied
by Sikh militants the Indian Prime Minister Indira
Gandhi (1917–1984) ordered it to be re-taken by
force. She was assassinated by her Sikh bodyguards
in retaliation and there were anti-Sikh riots all over
India in which Sikh men were killed and Sikh women
were raped. The Indian police in the Punjab then
began, or rather continued, to fight the secessionists
with terror. They are still using terror: Sikh men
have regularly been tortured to death by the police
and in 1992, eight years after Indira Gandhi's death,
a nineteen-year-old Sikh woman called Amandeep Kaur,
whose brother was suspected of terrorism, was arrested
and then allegedly raped and beaten in various police
stations. Shortly after she had complained and tried
to bring a case against the police, she was murdered,
either by the police or by their proxies. In the same
year a 24-year-old Sikh woman called Manjit Kaur[12]
was raped by policemen in her own home. She
was reportedly four months pregnant and was left

with scars on her cheeks after the policemen bit her repeatedly there.[13]

This kind of animalistic behaviour reminds us of something important about human beings that might help answer an important but ideologically dangerous question. Human beings are animals, that is, they have a biology, and that might help explain why the police in India are worse, on average, than the police in Britain or the US. Undoubtedly there are corruption and brutality in every police force on earth, but there are differences between individual policemen, differences between local police forces in individual countries, and differences between police forces in one country and police forces in another. The fact that there are also differences between one police force and the same police force at a different time immediately proves that culture is very important. It seems to be true, for example, that corruption and brutality were worse in the British police twenty or thirty years ago, when suspects were questioned much more violently than today and miscarriages of justice, although they are undoubtedly still occurring, were probably worse and more common. These changes presumably represent a change in culture, not in biology, though it may be difficult to separate the two: a kinder, gentler police force will attract kinder, gentler policemen, and kindness and gentleness are partly biological. Personality is partly based on physiology: extroverts seek stronger sensations than introverts because extroverts are physiologically different. For example, they may perceive sensations less strongly and so need stronger sensations to achieve the same level of satisfaction, or they may simply perceive sensations differently and be unconcerned at what introverts find unpleasant or disturbing: say, the pain and suffering of a tortured prisoner. They may also enjoy what introverts find unpleasant or disturbing: the pain and suffering of a tortured prisoner again.

There are of course huge variations of extroversion and introversion within races, but there may also be important variations between races. Many people do not think that 'race' is a respectable concept, of course, and certainly there are no absolute, qualitative differences between the biology of, say, the diverse light-skinned inhabitants of the British Isles and the biology of the diverse dark-skinned inhabitants of the Indian subcontinent. Nevertheless, there are biological tendencies that separate such groups on average: one famous example is lactose intolerance, that is, the inability of adults to digest a sugar called lactose found in raw milk. This intolerance is rare among northern Europeans, much less rare among northern Indians, and found in a majority of southern Indians: some rough estimates run at 5, 25 and 70 per cent respectively.[14] In other words, although it is impossible to assign an adult to a particular race based on their tolerance of lactose, it is certainly possible to say that they are more or less likely to belong to it. If they are able to digest lactose, they're more likely, though not certain, to be northern European; if they're not, they're more likely, though not certain, to be Indian.

However, inter-racial differences based on physiology, such as lactose intolerance, are much less controversial, perhaps because they're much less controvertible, than inter-racial differences based on psychology, such as differences in intelligence and criminality. Perhaps this is a lingering after-effect of Christianity: the intellectual and moral faculties are immaterial, like the soul, and are therefore supposed, like the soul, to float free of the body. It also seems very unjust that simply because one is born into a particular race one should have more or less chance of being intelligent or law-abiding, but to me it also seems perfectly possible. If one is born as a cat or a newt one is automatically deprived of the higher faculties, because the higher faculties, whatever Christianity or its ideological descendants may say, are based on biology. The philosopher Bertrand Russell once pointed out that no matter how eloquently a dog may bark, he cannot tell you his parents were poor but honest.[15] In other words, dogs cannot acquire language, because their genes do not code for the right sort of brain. Now, no one would deny that gross differences in human and canine genetics explain why human beings can and dogs can't speak, but many would deny that subtler differences in genetics might explain why, for example, there is greater corruption and brutality in the Indian and Pakistani police than in the British.

I don't see why this should be denied a priori, though it's important to stress that, like lactose intolerance, police corruption and brutality differ on average, not absolutely. If a policeman is corrupt and brutal he might be any race or nationality at all, he is simply more likely to be Indian or Pakistani than British. And perhaps this does have a genetic basis, though not necessarily a direct one. There are no genes coding for the taking of bribes or the use of torture, because those are both contingent expressions of culture and genes do not code directly for culture. Nevertheless, they code for some of what underlies culture, such as levels of testosterone. These differ widely, on average, between men and women, as well as between individual men, and that may help explain differences between male and female culture, as well as differences between the culture of some men and the culture of others. Male footballers have higher testosterone than female netball players, for example, and male rugby players have higher testosterone than male footballers. Similarly, male policemen, whether in India or Britain, presumably have higher testosterone than male clerks in either country: we are sorted into profession partly on the basis of things like levels of testosterone, although profession can also affect things like that and the authority enjoyed by policemen may in itself influence their physiology and psychology.

To observe this of members of the same race is relatively uncontroversial: on average, white policemen differ physiologically, and so psychologically, from white clerks. However, to observe this of members of different races is highly controversial: on average, British policemen differ physiologically, and so psychologically, from Indian policemen. But again, I don't see any reason for denying this a priori: there are differences, on average, between the ways the police behave in Britain and India, and this may be based on genetic differences between British and Indian policemen. Which isn't to offer excuses for police corruption and brutality in India or anywhere else: they can and should be reduced. Nevertheless, if you want to explain why the police are so much more corrupt and brutal in India, and in many other parts of the world, than in Britain, I can't see that examining culture can explain everything, because explaining differences in behaviour by differences in culture immediately raises the question of why cultures differ. Sometimes that question has been answered by climate in ways that remind us both how long these questions have existed and how differently they can be expressed. In the days when southern Muslim culture was clearly more advanced than northern Christian culture, a Muslim scholar called Massoud al-Massoud attributed this difference to the cold and damp of the sunless north, which bleached the skin and coarsened the sensibilities of races such as the Slavs, Franks and

Norsemen. Indeed, in the extreme north he reported that men were said to be like animals.[16]

Nowadays the suggestion is made in reverse: the higher the latitude, the richer and less corrupt the nation. Hence, the United Kingdom or the United States, in the north, is richer and less corrupt than Spain or Mexico, in the south. But do differences in climate cause differences in culture or are they simply correlated with differences in culture? Differences in climate are more directly related to differences in physiology, and there is a theory that northern Europeans, and particularly light-haired or blond northern Europeans, became more introverted because of the adaptations they made to cold. Higher levels of a neurotransmitter called norepinephrine help raise the body's temperature but simultaneously make the nervous system more reactive. If you perceive sensations more strongly, you tend to introversion: that is, you're naturally more timid. Does this explain the difference between northern and southern cultures in Europe? Does it explain not only differences in things generally associated with culture, such as music and art, but also differences in things like crime and corruption, which are part of culture too? Italy and Spain are more corrupt than the United Kingdom and, although this is sometimes attributed to differences in religion,[17] perhaps that has a partly genetic basis too. Why is Protestantism a northern religion? Do Protestant ideas – the importance of individual conscience and of postponing pleasure – naturally appeal more to introverted northern races? Or is Catholicism authoritarian because the extroverted southern races had to be tyrannised? Or both?

Support for these highly racist, highly controversial, but not necessarily wrong ideas comes from an observation made in the breeding of animals: that animals with darker fur are 'more tame and less instinctively timid'.[18] Tamer animals are less disturbed by the powerful stimuli of being handled and fed by human beings, that is, they're more extrovert. That psychological trait is ultimately a physiological one: it reflects chemical and perhaps anatomical differences in the nervous system. If the same differences are found in darker-skinned human beings, perhaps this explains differences in human culture, such as the greater corruption and brutality of the Indian and Pakistani police, and the greater corruption of Indian and Pakistani culture in general. In India, for example, it's possible to get a driving licence by paying a bribe without the inconvenience of having to sit a test,[19] which is not merely corrupt but highly anti-social too. But perhaps this sort of thing isn't general in Britain any more because Britain is far richer than India, and perhaps Britain is far richer than India because of colonialism: as well as pointing out the brutality of the Imperial Indian Police, George Orwell pointed out that:

> *the high standard of life we enjoy in England depends upon our keeping a tight hold on the Empire, particularly the tropical portions of it such as India and Africa. Under the capitalist system, in order that England may live in comparative comfort, a hundred million Indians must live on the verge of starvation – an evil state of affairs, but you acquiesce in it every time you step into a taxi or eat a plate of strawberries and cream.*[20]

Perhaps, as though a kind of heat-pump has been working, Britain has become socially warmer at India's expense.

But the question then arises of why Britain colonised India rather than the other way around. Could it just as easily have been the other way around but for some quirk of history, or was it more probable that Britain would conquer India, because the British ruling classes were more rapacious and warlike? If so, why, and does it necessarily contradict the purported introversion of the British?[21] Perhaps introverts make better soldiers because they're more disciplined; perhaps there are important genetic differences between the British classes. But if it was cultural, was it something to do with Christianity, which, unlike Indian Hinduism, is a missionary faith? After all, India had previously been conquered by the Moghals, who were followers of the missionary faith of Islam. Then again, the Raj was founded during the Enlightenment, which repudiated the idea that Christianity had absolute and exclusive truth, and at first the British were careful not to force their religion on their Indian subjects. When Christian evangelists began to change that in the nineteenth century, their Indian subjects responded with the Indian Mutiny of 1857, in which there were massacres and enormous cruelty by both sides. Like Partition, the Indian Mutiny reminds us that the recent past of the subcontinent contains violence unknown on the soil of mainland Britain since the English Civil War in the seventeenth century, and never known anywhere in Britain on the same scale. History is not a science and may never be, but it's certain that history in general is shaped by biology, because only human beings have a history: our genetic inheritance as human beings explains why we have art, literature, and police corruption. However, if the particular forms taken by history in different parts of the world are random, then perhaps the slightly differing genes of different racial groups have no influence and the growth of modern science, for example, could just as easily have taken place in India or China as in Europe.

Certainly some of the precursors of modern science arose in India and China, and India and China have accepted European science and made very important contributions to it, as proved by Indian and Chinese winners of the Nobel Prize. But could Indo-Sino-European science settle questions like why the police, who are imperfect everywhere, are more imperfect in India than they are in Britain? If science can and the answer is related to skin colour, Indian culture will have anticipated it just as Indian culture anticipated science in general. India has its own colour prejudices, which are most obvious in matrimonial advertisements: young Indian women, in particular, are careful to emphasise the lightness of their skin. Some historians suggest this is why Hindu deities like Kali have blue skin, which was a way of disguising the very dark or even black skin of India's original inhabitants, who were the original worshippers of deities such as Kali. These aboriginals are said to have been forced into lower castes by lighter-skinned invaders from the north who called themselves the *Arya* or 'noble ones' and whose name eventually, through the seemingly harmless science of linguistics, gave the Nazis the concept of the innately superior Aryan race.[22]

Concepts like that were refined in India much longer ago, however, and are still current in the so-called caste system that traditionally divides Hindu society into four groups: the *Brahmin*, or priests; the *Kshatriya*, or warriors; the *Vaisya*, or merchants; and the *Sudra*, or labourers. There are complicated sub-divisions of each caste too, but there is a further, literally out-caste group of Untouchables, so-called because their touch, and even their shadows, were believed to be ritually impure.

Mahatma Gandhi (1869–1948), trying to use supernaturalism to overturn the pernicious effects of supernaturalism, renamed them *Harijans* or 'God-People', but they are also known today, even among themselves, as *Dalits*, 'the Broken Ones'. Some of those who have always traditionally broken them are the police, in the same pattern as that seen in the United States during segregation: a light-skinned police force intimidating and sometimes even murdering members of a dark-skinned underclass. The Hindi word for caste, *varna*, can also mean 'colour', because skin colour traditionally fixes caste: the lighter one's skin, the higher one's caste, and so the darker, the lower. The Untouchables are so low as to fall outside the system of caste altogether, and so they have the darkest skins of all.

In this way India adds a final important ingredient to the recipe for bad cops: there are poverty, overcrowding and religious conflict, but there is also racial conflict. The police in pre-partition Ireland, and in post-partition Ulster, were notorious for mistreating Catholics, but they would almost certainly have been worse if Catholics and Protestants had been clearly different races as well as clearly different religions. To apply a prejudice quickly and efficiently, it's useful to have a quick way of identifying the group against which you are prejudiced. Skin colour is one of the quickest, but skin colour is nevertheless a very crude guide to the genetic patterns that almost certainly exist in the professions and arts. Within the so-called white inhabitants of Britain, for example, there are different genetic groups, and although the differences are very small, as they are between all human beings, they may also be very significant. One difference in fact is certainly significant: the Y chromosome that separates the genetic group known as men from the genetic group known as women. Whether on the subcontinent or elsewhere, it's men who are the bad cops – the ones beating and torturing suspects, raping women and children, extorting and accepting bribes, even hiring themselves out to commit murder.

That is obvious and, although there is no obvious explanation for it, it's an example of the way a difference in genetics translates into a gross difference in behaviour. To explain it culturally, as an example of men's different 'socialisation', doesn't fully explain the phenomenon, because culture does not appear out of nothing. If the difference between the genes of human beings and chimpanzees explains why human beings have police forces and chimpanzees don't, why does the difference between the genes of male and female human beings not explain part of why bad cops are overwhelmingly or even exclusively men, and bad nurses – the ones who injure or even murder their patients – often women? And why does the difference between the genes of British policemen and the genes of Indian policemen not help to explain why there are more and worse bad cops in India than in Britain? There's no doubt that, given the chance, many British policemen would happily torture and murder suspects to the extent, and beyond the extent, of some of their Indian counterparts, but the fact that they can't may say something about the genetic basis of the wider cultures in which the police of both countries work. It's impossible to say that the police are equally bad everywhere, and it's ridiculous to say that the police are bad anywhere simply because the police are, well, bad. There are explanations for the way they behave in any particular place at any particular time, and although genetics, in anything but the most general sense, may not be among them, it's impossible to dismiss it a priori. I question the idea of the police altogether – meant to stop crime, they not only create it, they often commit it too – but I still recognise that there are bad cops and there are worse cops, and trying to find out why India, Pakistan and Bangladesh have some of the worst cops in the world may help stop them being so bad. The first step to finding out why is to ask the question, and I don't want us to be scared off because some of the answers may involve skin colour and race. *Kaalii Māā*, the Black Mother of death who is actually blue, can teach us three interesting lessons. The first is that that colour can represent important things. The second is that labels based on colour can mislead. The third is that the power can be overturned and apparent weakness triumph over apparent strength, whether strength is represented by a divine husband or by bad cops or by ideologies that deny the importance of biology.

I'd like to thank Jack Sargeant for asking me to write this essay, for his help with it, and for not asking me to suppress my ideas (which he by no means shares).

BIBLIOGRAPHY
Mike Davis, *Late Victorian Holocausts: El Niño, Famines and the Making of the Third World*, Verso Books, London, 2000.

Peter Farb, *Word Play*, Jonathan Cape, London, 1974.

Duncan Forrest, ed., *A Glimpse of Hell: Reports on Torture Worldwide*, New York University Press, 1996.

Nicholas Goodrick-Clarke, *Black Sun: Aryan Cults, Esoteric Nazism and the Politics of Identity*, New York University Press, 2001.

Christopher Hitchens, *For the Sake of Argument: Essays and Minority Reports*, Verso Books, London, 1993.

Bernard Lewis, *The Muslim Discovery of Europe*, Phoenix Press, London, 2000.

George Orwell, *The Road to Wigan Pier*, Penguin Books, London, 1937.

Adam Parfrey, ed., *Apocalypse Culture*, Feral House, California, 1991.

Matt Ridley, *Genome: The Autobiography of a Species in 23 Chapters*, Fourth Estate, London, 1999.

Jack Sargeant, ed., *Death Cults*, Virgin Books, London, 2002.

NOTES

1. The stone appears to be a meteorite. See Hakim Bey's essay 'Instructions for the Kali Yuga' in Adam Parfrey's *Apocalypse Culture* (1991).

2. The pronunciation in English is a mistake based on the transliteration from the Devanagari alphabet: *thug* is pronounced like the English word 'tug', but with stronger aspiration: *t'hug*.

3. For further details of the Thugs, see Chris Barber's essay in *Death Cults* (2002), ed. Jack Sargeant, in the Virgin True Crime series.

4. *The Road to Wigan Pier* (1937), ch. 9.

5. On Jewish support for Hitler, see Christopher Hitchens, *For the Sake of Argument: Essays and Minority Reports* (1993) or www.disinfo.com/pages/article/id1126/pg1/.

6. See www.abc.net.au/rn/science/ockham/stories/s19040.htm and Mike Davis's *Late Victorian Holocausts: El Niño, Famines and the Making of the Third World* (2000).

7. It's also an acronym of the regions making up West Pakistan: Punjab, Afghania, Kashmir, Iran, Sindh, Tukharistan, Afghanistan and Baluchistan.

8. Nevertheless, the Pakistani military dictatorship under President Yahya Khan (1917–80), like the military dictatorship responsible for similar

massacres in Indonesia from 1965 to 1966, continued to receive military aid from the United States. See www.gendercide.org/case_bangladesh.html for further details.

9. See www.asyl.net/Magazin/Docs/docs-17/L-28/L9343bgd.htm.

10. See www.amnesty.org.uk/news/mag/may99/children.html.

11. See *A Glimpse of Hell: Reports on Torture Worldwide* (1996), ed. Duncan Forrest.

12. Just as all Sikh men use the surname Singh, meaning 'Lion', all Sikh women use the surname Kaur, meaning 'Princess'.

13. See www.maboli.com/Sikh_HR/Picture_Gallery/rape_victims.html.

14. See for example www.notmilk.com/wbstance.html.

15. Apparently quoted by Peter Farb in *Word Play* (1974).

16. See Bernard Lewis's *The Muslim Discovery of Europe* (2000), which is quoted at www.sammustafa.com/WorldReadings/crusaders.html.

17. There is a theory that Catholic regions in Europe are more corrupt than Protestant ones: for example, corruption in Germany is said to be worse in the Catholic south.

18. Matt Ridley, *Genome: The Autobiography of a Species in 23 Chapters* (1999), 'Chromosome 11: Personality'.

19. See www.india-reform.org/articles/corruption.html.

20. *The Road to Wigan Pier* (1937), ch. 9.

21. One interesting theory is that the European staple wheat, which requires much less attention than the Asian staple rice, allowed Europeans more leisure to wage war.

22. Northern Indian languages like Hindi and Bengali are related to nearly all European languages, and

this language family was once called the Aryan family. When the term Aryan was discredited by the Nazis, it was replaced with the more transparent term Indo-European. See Nicholas Goodrick-Clarke's *Black Sun: Aryan Cults, Esoteric Nazism and the Politics of Identity* (2001) for further details of the Nazi interest in Hinduism.

11. THE WAY OF FLESH

EXTRACTING CONFESSIONS BY TORTURE: AN OVERVIEW
Jack Sargeant

The following does not focus on one specific case, nor one specific species of corrupt police officer, nor on one particular country or period of policing. Rather, it seeks to present a selection of miscellaneous abuses meted out on to the bodies of those who have come unwittingly into contact with the powers of the law around the world.

As soon as a suspect becomes the focus of legal investigation, arrest and detainment, his/her body becomes an object under the control of the State. The subject becomes merely an object on which power can be enacted. All freedoms, however relative, are removed. Everything from physical needs (diet, toiletry requirements, exercise and so on) to articulation and speech become dictated by the authorities of law. The following notes only offer the briefest outline of some of the brutal and sickening methods by which that body has been controlled.

Torture has a long history, with, in the West, both the Catholic Church[1] and the State wallowing in the bruised, bloody, twisted, ruined remains of the victims whose bodies were beaten, broken, cut, sliced, smashed, abused, raped, hacked, dismembered and burned in order to facilitate the process of justice – either God's or the State's.

Historically, for the State, the spectacle of torture and execution was the spectre of justice. Massive crowds would watch as the law was enacted. Justice in action:

the stocks, whippings, brandings, hangings, beheadings, mutilations and deaths, all served both to demonstrate the brutal and swift justice of the State against transgressors and satisfy the public's desire for seeing punishment; for paying witness to the law in action. Moreover, such spectacles served to remind the masses exactly what happened to those who broke the law.[2] But often the spectacle of seeing the results of breaking the law was looked upon as something of a family day out. In eighteenth-century London one could enjoy a home-baked meat pie from the vendor's cart while watching the necks snap at Tyburn.

While our brutal, primitive ancestors freely admitted to the activity of obtaining a 'confession' through physical and coercive means, in the modern world legislation exists to outlaw and illegalise torture. Although it would be wrong to assume that all cultures and societies follow identical laws, it should be observed that the Universal Declaration of Human Rights, Article 5, clearly states: 'No one shall be subjected to torture or to cruel, inhuman or degrading treatment or punishment.'[3]

The illegality of torture means that few countries ever admit to supporting it, although according to Amnesty International torture occurs in more than 111 countries[4] and was widespread in more than 70 countries between 1997 and 2000.[5] The number of refugees claiming to have been victims of, or witnesses to, torture would appear to substantiate these figures. There is an increased recognition among medical professionals that specific physical and psychological traumas may follow torture, and that with the correct support and treatment victims can be helped to deal with both the physical and psychological aspects of their abuse.[6]

The following is a survey of available information from numerous sources;[7] notably this is only information relating to human rights abuses following arrest and during interrogation by police forces and/or those charged with responsibility for law enforcement. The following excludes the conditions of those found 'guilty' and imprisoned, and on-going torture/human rights abuses once the convicted prisoner finds himself/herself stranded within the confines of the prison system.

The police use various methods of obtaining confessions of 'guilt' from detainees. The following is by no means a complete list of the tortures that are commonly used, with notes on specific infamous local variations.

The most simple – and easiest to 'justify' – manifests in the form of beatings. In some cases beatings are comparatively minor, the suspect whacked around the head with a telephone directory, leaving no mark. The technique hurts, and repeated hits can result in the dizzying nausea that is concussion. A variation of this technique sees the suspect having a mattress thrown over them and the cops jumping on the mattress – hurting the detainee, and even risking deep organ damage, while leaving the flesh unbruised.

Torturers commonly engage in *telefone*, the beating of the ears to cause deafness and concussion, and *falanga*, the beating of the soles of the feet. Vicious beatings involve punching and kicking the victim even as he lies on the floor in a foetal position, cop boots finding their target in the delicate tissue of the kidneys, as well as the back and head. Cracked ribs, concussion and bruising. Beatings are commonplace in much of the world, truncheons and nightsticks swinging on to suspects' heads and limbs are a daily occurrence, but there are some who have turned beatings into an art.

In Chechnya there are reports that those arrested are forced to run the human corridor, a double line of cops swinging their clubs and bashing the arrestees, their truncheons pummelling the tender – and often already damaged – flesh of detainees as they are moved into detention centres. A human corridor of twenty cops – ten on each side – using their full strength to swing a truncheon into the detainee's body, thus guaranteeing at least twenty nasty hits. Such is the brutality of these police officers that there are reports of a retarded fourteen-year-old boy being forced to run this nightmarish corridor. Witnesses detail that on occasion those already injured – sometimes seriously – are also subjected to this ritualised beating.[8] This is the abuse of cop power.

In those countries where there is less chance of being found out, where the grind of daily existence lurches through suffocating poverty, cops are even more likely to develop extreme methods of brutal beatings unhindered by journalists or human rights workers. Allied to political leaders, or tribal leaders, or betraying guerrilla links, cops in third world and developing countries can get away with so much more, using not just truncheons, but also boards with nails in. Bats. Iron bars. Steel cables. Whips. Full-scale bone-breaking, skin-splitting, muscle-ripping, exploded-organ, crushed-nose, blinding beatings.

Humans being reduced to jellied sacks of smashed, pulped flesh.

But there are other ways to inflict beatings. Other ways in which pain can be ruthlessly deployed on to a human body.

Like the psychopathic inquisitors of the mediaeval world, modern cops understand the value of suspension.

Hanging the victim from a pole.

Hanging the victim from a hook.

Hanging the victim from a beam.

Suspending them above the ground.

Each country has its own particular favourite method. In some, the tips of the toes may be allowed to just touch the floor, with the arms twisted behind the body and handcuffed or otherwise fixed to a beam. Hanging from arms suspended at the wrists – depriving the hands of blood even as the shoulders become dislocated, muscle, bone and tissue savagely tearing, bruising and swelling.[9]

Suspensions allow the torturers the convenience of being able to beat the suspects without affording the victim the possibility of turning or twisting their body to deflect or protect themselves from the repeated heavy blows. They also enable the cops responsible for the interrogation to focus the punches or kicks on particular parts of the body. Once again the kidneys are said to be a favoured target – their sensitivity, and relatively exposed position, making them ideal for inflicting pain; moreover, sustained beatings on the kidneys is likely to cause permanent damage. Permanent health problems. The victim will suffer physical discomfort for the rest of their lives.

In parts of Brazil these suspensions have reportedly occurred in specially constructed torture rooms, which are an alleged feature of many police stations. These rooms feature shower hoses and electrical outlets, but the central aspect is the perch, from which these torture rooms get their name: *Sala de Pau*. The detainee is handcuffed over the beam, his/her knees bent over the perch, leaving the head pointing downwards. Not only is this the ideal position for beating a suspect, but it also enables the interrogator to indulge in various forms of water torture, forcing water into the face. Forcing water into the mouth. Forcing water up the nose. The victim is unable to turn away. To escape. Reports of those who have undergone such degrading punishments suggest that the victim believes that he/she is suffocating, drowning.[10]

Across the world there is evidence that those who are arrested may also undergo electric shock treatment, sometimes via cattle prods, sometimes via hand-cranked shock devices that shoot electricity into the body via clamps placed on the ears.

On the lips.

On the neck.

On the nipples.

On the testicles.

On the penis.

In the anus.

And in the vagina.

If flesh allows a clamp, or is tender, or is sensitive, it will be subject to electrical torture. Shocks sending suspended victims into convulsions and unconsciousness.

Only to come around and find that the nightmare continues.

For hours.

For days.

For as long as the cops think it should.

There are other methods of torture. Asphyxiation is commonplace in many countries, with the victim having a plastic bag or mask put over his/her head. Not only does the victim feel that they are suffocating, but often they will be simultaneously beaten, forced to hyperventilate. Their lungs bursting for air. The alveoli exploding for oxygen. Desperate to breathe, yet unable to inhale. Until the torturer allows them to breathe. Gasping for air. Barely able to breathe before once again being suffocated. Again and again.

Other forms of asphyxiation are more grotesque. More brutal (if brutality can be quantifiable, if pain and humiliation and blind terror can be measured). In Israel the preferred method of 'suffocation' interrogation used by the internal security service (the Shin Bet) involved putting a wet sack over the detainee's head and blasting the detainee with loud music. In an added twist, the sack covering the victim's head would be soaked in urine. The method is known as the Shabach.[11]

In some countries the head may be submerged in a bucket of water.

The head may be dunked in a bucket of urine.

The head may be forced into a bucket of sewage.

The victim is forced to choke on human faeces.[12]

In many countries sexual abuse and rape are common forms of torture. Sometimes suspects are naked while being tortured, humiliation contributing to the process of physical degradation. Unwashed, bruised bodies laughed at and commented on by the inquisitors. Sometimes this can go further, with the naked cowering victim being forced to hear his/her[13] tormentors debate whether or not they will rape the victim.[14]

Often torturers will rape women with foreign objects, forcing everything from police nightsticks to glass bottles into their vaginas. In the Ivory Coast there were reports of women being penetrated with police truncheons and having sand forced into their vaginas.[15] Other reports detail women having chillies or hot pepper pushed into their vaginas.[16] Sometimes women are gang raped. Sometimes these rapes go on for days.

And there's more. Suspects may be burned with cigarettes.

Burned on their nipples.

Burned on their genitals.

Burned on the soles of their feet.

Sometimes victims are forced to walk over burning tyres.

Sometimes they have melting plastic dripped on to their flesh.

And still there is more. Torturers may rub chilli in victims' eyes.

Or remove teeth – yanking them from the gums.

Or pull fingernails using pliers.

Or cut flesh.

Or even skin the victim alive – pulling thin strips of flesh from the detainee's body.

Or amputate the prisoner's digits one at a time.

Or crush the victim's testicles.

Or castrate the victim.

But torture does not have to be purely physical. Torture can be psychological. The very essence of torture is psychological. Torture one detainee in front of others and the rest may confess to anything the interrogator wants them to; to anything the interrogator *needs* them to. If one person is forced to witness the torture of another, he or she knows that if they do not comply, they too may be tortured. Some torturers may even make victims torture each other. In the blood-splattered interrogation room anything becomes possible.

Psychological torture can be used to create sheer terror. A terror that makes victims wet themselves. A terror that makes victims scream and beg that they will sign *anything*, confess to *any* crime. Mock executions see the victims dragged from their cells, genuinely believing they are going to die. Other psychological abuses consist of telling detainees that their loved ones will be tortured. Dragging people from their cells, people who have already witnessed or suffered torture and telling them that their wives will be raped. Their husbands will be raped. There are cases of torturers telling people that they will torture and rape their children.[17]

But psychological abuse extends beyond threats of execution and torture. To those imprisoned in torture centres – in police headquarters, army bases, detainment centres or secret locations – witnessing torture daily has its own psychological toll. Prisoners are forced to hear the screams of pain and the pleading for mercy of other detainees. Prisoners are forced to witness the bloody bodies of their fellow inmates dragged from the torture chamber.

Indeed, the entire process of arrest and incarceration in much of the world is itself a form of torture, with many suspects being kept prisoner without trial, and often without charges, for weeks or even months. Moreover, these prisoners may be kept in unsanitary and overcrowded conditions.

Forced to share cells with many more people than the cell was designed to hold.

Forced to share cells with no bedding.

Forced to share cells with no heating.

Forced to share cells with only a bucket to shit in.

Forced to share cells without even the luxury of a bucket to piss in.

Often psychological abuse takes the form of depriving detainees of contact with the outside world, blindfolding them when moving them throughout the prison.

Putting them in cells with no window.

Putting them in cells with no light.

Or with the light on continually. 24 hours a day – day after day after day.

Sensory deprivation is common.

Psychological abuse can consist of depriving prisoners of sleep, sometimes for days at a time, pushing them closer to nervous collapse, psychological breakdown, and even death. Sometimes detainees are forced to stand still for hours.

Or sit handcuffed to a chair for hours. Or forced to sit in an unnatural position for hours. Unable to sleep, the muscles screaming to relax, or move, forcing the prisoner to undergo cramping agonies.

And then there is insanity: entire worlds gone amok; all rationality cast aside.

In news reports which detail the world-turned-upside-down, where all evidence of humanity is erased, flensed like tissue from bone. In this world, cops or other representatives of 'justice' and 'law' descend to the state of utter monstrous abjection. Where the blackest, nastiest fantasies of power are given free rein. This is a world without logic, without reason, a world where the feral nature of cops – of humanity – is given free rein.

Where detainees are thrown into open sewers, to swim (or drown) in human faeces.[18]

Where those that are arrested are forced to eat their own excrement.[19]

Where those that are arrested are forced to drink their own blood.[20]

Where those that are arrested are forced into eating human flesh.

Where those that are arrested are forced into cannibalising their own relatives. This is truly a world gone insane, a world utterly unimaginable. Yet such atrocities have occurred,[21] and no doubt they will occur again.

This is the legacy of law. This is the role of torture. And the screams will not stop.

REFERENCES
Clare Dyer, 'Pinochet "Led Chile Tortures" ', *The Guardian*, 19 January 1999, www.guardian.co.uk.

Sally James, 'Two Years In The Life of a Former Dictator', *The Guardian*, 3 March 2000, www.guardian.co.uk

John Sweeney, 'Greed And Torture at the House of Saud', *The Observer*, 24 November 2002, www.observer.co.uk

Harvey M Weinstein, MD, MPH, Laura Dansky, PhD, and Vincent Iacopino, MD, Phd, 'Torture and War Trauma Survivors in Primary Care Practice', *Survivors International*, www.survivorsintl.org/info/primarycare. html

'No Trade Off Between Human Rights and Security: Amnesty International Outlines Human Rights Violations in 152 Countries', *Amnesty International Report 2002*, AI Index: POL 10/006/2002, www.amnesty.org

'Turkey: Endemic Torture Must End Immediately', www.amnesty.org

'Philippines: Persistence of Torture In The Philippines', Amnesty International Press Release, AI Index, ASA 35/003/2003, dated 24/01/2003, www.amnesty.org.

'UN Condemns DR Congo Cannibalism', 15 January 2003, BBC News, http://news.bbc.co.uk www.bbc.co.uk

World: Middle East Israeli 'Torture' Methods Illegal, BBC News, Monday 6 September 1999.

'Worldwide Torture on the Rise', the *Guardian*, 19 October 2000, www.guardian.co.uk.

Human Rights Watch, 'Memorandum to the U.S Government Regarding Religious Persecution In Uzbekistan', 10 August 2001, http://hrw.org/backgrounder/eca/uzbek-aug/torture.htm).

Human Rights Watch, ' "Welcome to Hell", Arbitrary Detention, Torture, and Extortion in Chechnya', www.hrw.org/reports

Human Rights Watch, 'Behind Bars In Brazil', www.hrw.org/reports98/brazil

Human Rights Watch, 'Cote D'Ivoire: the New Racism: The Political Manipulation of Ethnicity in Cote D'Ivoire', www.hrw.org/reports/2001/ivorycoast

Human Rights Watch, 'Justice Undermined: Balancing Security and Human Rights in the Palestinian Justice System', www.hre.org/reports/2001/pa/index

'Confessions At Any Cost – Police Torture In Russia', www.hrw.org/campaigns/russia/torture/methods.htm www.remember-chile.org.uk/beginners

NOTES

1. During the Spanish Inquisition – which ran from 1478 until 1834 – thousands were tortured and murdered by the Catholic Church. For the Church, torture marked a way in which to extricate a confession of guilt (invariably, no other confession could ever be valid); public executions of those sinners found guilty of heresy and witchcraft served as a reminder of a vengeful God's omnipotent power.

   Historically, torture was not just a process in which the victim would be forced into making a confession, the mortification of flesh was also part of the process of punishment – specific torturers were designed to extract a precise confession: those accused of sodomy would be anally abused; those women accused of consorting with the Devil, or his minions, sexually, or of sexual impropriety, would be vaginally tortured. Devices were designed specifically for these sins, most infamously the vaginal, oral and anal pear. This steel pear-shaped object was designed to be pushed into the relevant body cavity and, via a screw mechanism, slowly opened, expanding within the cavity and – thanks to its sharpened edges – shredding the tender walls of the arsehole, or ripping the soft tissue of the cervix and vagina, or cracking and smashing the teeth. Likewise, women accused of nagging would be punished and tortured simultaneously by being forced to wear metal scolds-briddles, devices that strapped around the head while forcing a piece of metal into the mouth in order to stop the female from talking.

There were also more generally implements of physical abuse, designed to crush and break bones, dislocate joints, bruise and tear muscles, rip ligaments and savage tissue. The strappado, which suspended the victim in strange positions a few feet from the ground, then dropped them – jarring bone and muscle. The rack, which stretched the victims' bodies, and the wheel on which victims would have their limbs broken. Fingers and toes could be crushed in thumbscrews while heads could be crushed in the skull splitter. Other devices were designed to maim via the destruction of flesh – the spider (aka the Spanish Spider) which was designed to mangle, crush and tear off the victim's testicles or breasts. More specific was the breast ripper – ostensibly a massive cutting and crushing device analogous to gigantic scissors. The Cat's Paw (aka the Spanish Tickler) was a series of blades designed to cut and rip flesh and muscle, tearing tissue to the bone. A variety of specialised devices were designed to cut flesh, remove tongues and enucleate eyes. Justice and punishment were blood splattered.

2. Such violence appears to have been universal – with brutal public execution and torture as prevalent in Eastern as Western countries.

3. The Universal Declaration of Human Rights was adopted by the United Nations on 10 December 1948 (General Assembly resolution 217 a (III). The full text is available online at www.web.amnesty. org/web/aboutai.nsf and http://193.194.138.190/ udhr/lang/eng.htm). There have been numerous other Acts against torture passed; notably, however, some governments actually vote against this – perhaps preferring a world in which torture may exist.

4. 'No Trade Off Between Human Rights and Security: Amnesty International Outlines Human Rights Violations in 152 Countries', *Amnesty International Report 2002*, AI Index: POL 10/006/2002 (www. amnesty.org).

5. 'Worldwide Torture on the Rise', the *Guardian*, 19 October 2000, www.guardian.co.uk.

6. These are manifested through physical signs such as: scars from burns, beatings and whippings, musculoskeletal and nerve injuries from suspensions, and sexual dysfunction from genital trauma. Psychological effects include post-traumatic stress disorder, anxiety, depression and psychosis, among others.

7. Amnesty International (www.amnesty.org) and Human Rights Watch (www.hrw.org) have large online databases. Both organisations are committed to working for human rights, campaigning for human rights, and researching and exposing human rights violations. Amnesty International is a worldwide campaigning movement that works to promote internationally recognised human rights. Human Rights Watch is dedicated to protecting the human rights of people around the world.

8. Human Rights Watch, '"Welcome to Hell",

Arbitrary Detention, Torture, and Extortion in Chechnya', www.hrw.org/reports

9. In Russia such suspensions are known colloquially as the *lastochka* or the swallow ('Confessions At Any Cost – Police Torture In Russia', www.hrw.org/campaigns/russia/torture/methods.htm). Such suspensions have also been used by the Palestinian security forces (Human Rights Watch, 'Justice Undermined: Balancing Security and Human Rights in the Palestinian Justice System', www.hre.org/reports/2001/pa/index.htm ~ TopOfPage), the Saudi secret police (John Sweeney, 'Greed And Torture at the House of Saud', *The Observer*, 24 November 2002, www.observer.co.uk) and the Turkish police ('Turkey: Endemic Torture Must End Immediately', http://www.amnesty.org), among many others.

10. Human Rights Watch, 'Behind Bars In Brazil', www.hrw.org/reports98/brazil.

11. World: Middle East Israeli 'Torture' Methods Illegal, BBC News, Monday 6 September 1999, http://news.bbc.co.uk/1/hi/world/middle east/439554.stm. Following condemnation for creating a method of abuse that degrades and suffocates the suspect, the state declared it would make an effort to find a 'ventilated' sack.

12. Asphyxiation via a plastic bag, or mask, is known as dry submarino, while the use of buckets of fluid or semi-liquid substances is known as wet submarino.

13. Although it is more common for women to be raped by torturers – or those working on their behalf – male rape also occurs.

14. Under the right-wing dictatorship of General Pinochet in Chile many suspects suffered torture,

including rape, and, in a chilling twist, stories emerged that some were raped by specially trained dogs (see Clare Dyer, 'Pinochet "Led Chile Tortures"', the *Guardian*, 19 January 1999, and Remember Chile, www.remember-chile.org.uk/beginners). Following the end of his rule Pinochet moved to England, where he was supported by various powerful people, not least former Conservative Prime Minister Margaret Thatcher who in January 1999 defended his human rights record (see Sally James, 'Two Years In The Life of a Former Dictator', *The Guardian*, 3 March 2000).

15. Human Rights Watch, 'Cote D'Ivoire: the New Racism: The Political Manipulation of Ethnicity in Cote D'Ivoire', www.hrw.org/reports/2001/ivorycoast/index

16. Such torture has been documented in the Philippines ('Philippines: Persistence of Torture In The Philippines', Amnesty International Press Release, AI Index, ASA 35/003/2003, dated 24/01/2003, www.amnesty.org) as well as in Kenya ('Worldwide Torture on the Rise', *The Guardian*, 19 October 2000, www.guardian.co.uk).

17. Such cases have been reported in, for example, Uzbekistan (see: Human Rights Watch, 'Memorandum to the US Government Regarding Religious Persecution In Uzbekistan', 10 August 2001, http://hrw.org/backgrounder/eca/uzbek-aug/torture.htm).

18. As happened on the Ivory Coast.

19. The Ivory Coast – in events that happened at the National Police Academy, National Gendarme Academy, and the Agban Gendarme Camp (source: www.hrw.org/reports/2001/ivorycoast).

20. The Ivory Coast (source: www.hrw.org/reports/2001/ivorycoast).

21. Most recently in the Democratic Republic of Congo, where rebel forces took over various communities (see: 'UN Condemns DR Congo Cannibalism', 15 January 2003, BBC News, http://news.bbc.co.uk).

12. FORCE VERSUS THEORY

PROTECT AND SERVE. THE SHIP IS SINKING

Lance Sinclair

The weak can either be persecuted or protected. In an obvious analogy, they can be herded, slaughtered, milked, raped or nursed to a comfortable old age. It is up to the shepherd of the weak to keep watch for predators that may use his flock to serve their own nefarious ends. Between the carer and the black, wet-toothed wraith is where the chess game for the blood and viscera of the innocent is played out.

Asking the sheep their opinion on the tactics of their keepers, or the treatment of an attacker whose intentions and methods they've been blissfully sheltered from, is surely the fanciful notion of a mind having laboured under the umbrella of comfort and the privilege of theory for too long a spell.

A mind never exposed to the unblinking face of brutality, nor its steady hand. It is not comfortable for us to rationalise violence. Violence, almost always the end product of confusion, is at least pure and clear: it is. There is no argument to be made for it or against it. It is as cleansing and as terrible as fire. How can one who wilfully avoids conflict to the extent that they no longer have even a genetic trace memory of extreme behaviour judge the actions of the faceless mass they send in to deal with the front line of their white bread, socially created war? Cops are what stop you from being eaten alive by the neighbour who doesn't cotton on to your liberal, bookworm ways. Their existence stops a dope-hungry teenager from busting your mother's hip when he throws her over the bus stop seat by her ankles and snatches her purse. It is the cops that will at least give pause to the drooling, slobbering, weakling rapist and the sloppy, mean, stupid drunk.

If white, predominately Western society were to be presented as corpus, it is one who has come to distrust the pain receptors that warn the brain of physical injury, to be sceptical of the actions of antibodies and their motives in protecting the body. A brain in denial over the state of its shell.

Are we so far distanced from the basic, genetic animal truth of ourselves that justice writ in pain truly repels us? Not on a theoretic level, of the kind that one politely dances around while conversing with other liars about humanistic concerns. That kind of hypocrisy is expected and indulged in by most, but the real truth, when we are alone or with true confidantes: does the police brutality that you are exposed to via third- or fourth-hand reports make the gut recoil in horror, or relax in the knowledge that the fortress of rationalisation and politeness is still being secured at its dangerous out-skirts?

Society creates a large amount of the pressures and injustices that lead people to turn to crime. True. We are all a part of this machine. Only complete and total violent revolution would be able to turn our ugly, bloated, smug capitalist survival-of-the-fattest treadmill around. Police are the identifiable front line face of the fist of this system. True. Who among us would be able to lead this overthrow without succumbing to corruption and the narcotic of power? What would we replace the current regime with? What is an acceptable level of violence to be benchmarked for revolutionary purposes? If a few 'innocents' get lined up against the wall and off-ed, won't it be in the interest of a greater good? What is to be done about those who may disagree, or better, those who care for nothing but their own fleeting desires and needs? The ones who will, as they do now, operate outside any framed plan? There are more among us who live in a world of corrupt, murderous lusts and delicious evil than any cursory wave of the torch of concern can make out. Wolves. Bacteria. Fire. Invulnerable to theory or polite rationale.

We are painted into a comfortable corner of our own making.

THE VOLUNTARY CASTRATO

That august tome *The Encyclopaedia Britannica* describes the typical practice of community-based law enforcement in Anglo-Saxon England:

> *When crimes were observed, citizens were expected to raise an alarm, gather their countrymen, and pursue and capture the criminal. All citizens were obliged to pursue wrongdoers, and those who refused were subject to punishment. If a crime was committed with no witnesses, efforts to identify the criminal after the fact were the responsibility of the victim alone: no governmental agency existed for the investigation and solution of crimes.*

While the condemnation of police brutality is widespread, the demonisation of vigilante behaviour is an even more popular viewpoint. An organised police force in Western society is a relatively new development. A few hundred years have made the world of difference.

What we see described above is mob rule, as we would now call it. In simpler times, in a community based around agriculture, operating in a self-sufficient manner, with population at a level of practical sanity, this made sense. If burning jealousy or petty squabbles might lead to the framing of an innocent citizen with no legal recourse, then so be it. Flawed, but practical, and no doubt applicable to the circumstances. Now, in a world supposedly leagues beyond the simple toiling farming community, the idea of pursuing and punishing a criminal is anathema to our advanced sensibilities. Should a citizen, attacked by vicious assailants while making his way home on public transport, gun down those attackers with what he believes to be appropriate force, he will not only be the target of critical speculation by the liberal media, but also be forced to compensate anyone who he, out of foolish pity or simple misjudgement, allowed to live. The writing is clear: we, as a species have now decided that this type of behaviour is now inappropriate.

Fair enough.

Chasing an urchin into the town square and stoning the poor skinny little blighter to death for stealing some corn is not how we do things now. Society has become far more complicated, as, apparently, have we. No longer do we live in isolated pockets of community where faces are familiar and motives easily discerned. The desire for *more* permeates our polluted modern souls. Drugs, possessions, sex, power. They all equal happiness, and they all equal going beyond. Pushing constantly against the walls of ourselves, tearing outwards from the shell of misery that isolates us. Are we miserable from the inside or the outside? Is the craving for *more* the product of an ego and a mind desperately reaching for newer highs and goals to fill the internal existential void, or do we want these things only because we keep having them rubbed in our faces by the society we willingly wallow in, like swine in their trough, as the answers to the tragedy of living in a world that has no real problems?

Crime, the reasons for it and the kaleidoscope of acts it defines have changed during the twentieth century. Man now has time to reflect and dream and theorise. The human animal now has a universe of extreme temptation and a soul emptier than he has ever known. It is a flawed utopia that we have accepted, that we have made and, through our apathy and lack of change, given approval to, and one that is enforced through flawed rules.

We have appointed a force of our own, especially trained and selected, to act as the dam, the dyke, the sea wall against the tide of our self-created sins. Through lack of education, lack of available resources, and the false promise of unlimited wish fulfilment, we have created modern crime. We, the average citizens, are unable to cope with its unreasoning, red eyes and cruel, snatching hands. Professionals have been created. We call them the police. The village no longer has the trust between its citizens that it once had. Who now would join a neighbour in hot furious pursuit of their perceived attacker? Who even knows their neighbours? The modern world is desire unfulfilled. To beat back the sheer, crying, needing force of that requires people that are willing to go into places the majority of us do not have the heart to. For us to judge their tactics, motivations or deeds is just another privilege that they provide for us.

THE BUTTERFLY THEORY
But what about individual cases and examples? Life isn't as simple as broad strokes across a global canvas. There are countless individual cases in which the rights of one person have been shaken like the rabbit whose neck is held tight in the salivating jaws of a brutal dog and snapped with such a quiet and sudden jerk that only

through a close and unrelenting vigil can we hope to protect the freedom of the individual.

Go ahead. There are plenty of mean, selfish cops, and a small percentage that are bone-deep corrupt. The word 'evil' would be easy to apply, if the author felt sanctimonious enough to label others with a vague, slightly metaphysical medieval term just as likely to be applied to himself, should the critic's podium be sufficiently sanctimonious and distanced.

The crack at the heart of this view is one established in bedrock far older than we. Modern thought, creator of corruption, doubt and guilt, gives us the belief that we are all special. Every individual snowflake has its own destiny, its own purpose and its own will. We are not the blank, white blizzard or pulpy, congealing mass of precipitance. We (read 'Me' or 'I') count for something, even though the world is more bloated with our tired, lazy, corpulent species than it ever has been. There are billions of us, feeding from the same limited diet of possibility and option, yet the individual will persist, to the grim, bloody-knuckled end in the insistence that he counts.

Believing that others matter is the easiest step and biggest building block in establishing faith in the self. Not 'others' in the sense of those we choose to involve in our lives, to care for, and have care for us, but the 'other' that makes up the amorphous, endlessly varied yet stultifying uniform face of the world. They're all just theory. Their losses, success, or simple, flat-lined lives should mean as much to you as yours does to them. Watching one's own back is the most basic law of survival, one of many that is being replaced with more vague, esoteric, fleeting concerns. Instead of directing the obvious need for the planet to advance and improve in the only direction that counts, inwards, we are avoiding the most obvious and direct path to action by focusing on the esoteric and conceptual. Window dressing on a tenement slum. The true humanist can improve this world by improving themselves, by being a better, more considerate, more direct and honest person. Alternatively, they can bury their real selves under safe, clichéd dogma. Being part of any team with a catchy slogan will do wonders for those with low self-esteem or a fractured concept of 'place'.

Witness the unwashed multitudes that would tie themselves to threatened trees, as long as the media is there to bear witness, and their filthy, gas-belching vans able to transport them.

Witness the feminist, humanist radical whose heroin habit financially fuels the dictatorship of continents they'll never visit.

Witness the critic of police brutality who would cry tears for seventeen-year-old Andre Burgess, shot and killed by police while reaching for a candy bar, which was mistaken for a firearm, or Rodney King, whose beating at the hands of peace officers was captured on video tape and catalysed into a topic of global discussion. People who would jump under a fucking dumpster if either of these black males approached them on a darkened street.

We're living in a snitch nation now, pretending to care while merely inflating our own feelings of well-being and experience with the selected details of other lives that fit into the tired puzzle of our manufactured id. As though there weren't thousands of others with your exact same profile.

Police brutality: how absurd that we would even pretend to care.

YOU DON'T HAVE TO SAY PLEASE

Your fate is to lose, because you are distracted. You are distracted by your illusions of goodwill, you are distracted by your sense of fair play and you are distracted by your indignation at a world that remains so unfair and so inconsistent in its treatment of the downtrodden. Justice and righteousness are artificial constructs created by thinking man to make us feel profound or deified when carrying out the most basic societal tasks of evaluation and punishment. We distanced ourselves from the dirty work of having to pass judgement and deal with the personal repercussions of such by appointing the strongest examples of our clan this task. Misplaced guilt – the guilt of the pampered that is nothing but tired luxury – as well as the spring of morbid curiosity in our hearts that will seemingly never dry up, force us to peer behind the curtain of peacekeeping, to reveal snatches of the killing floor providing the food of freedom. Uncomfortable with the trace memory of pain and conflict we are trying to breed out, we are upset by the use of force when viewed in any context, even one beyond our understanding. Pity is waste, for those who express it, and even more so for those who are the target of it.

As long as there is a semblance of spirit left in us, there will be those deemed to be the oppressors and those deemed to be the victims. There is no right or wrong choice to make, it is not a theory that one needs to have faith in: a fact requires no faith. As members of the contemporary Western world, we are sitting on the top of the pile. Our ancestors chose the role of oppressor for us. This is a world populated by child kings, waited on and cared for. The price of victory tastes like copper in this mouth, spoon fed and wiped by undying mothers. White guilt. Those not in your position hate you for that weakness, so much that you don't want to know the extent of the war being waged to ensure your continued restless comfort. Only this kind of confused, petulant child would clumsily attempt to undermine its own guards.

Are you blind? Do you live in or near any major metropolitan city? Are you really so full of this self-loathing death wish that you would welcome the last chaotic, viral overthrow of your precipitous status? Your storm troopers and their presence allow you the privilege of human behaviour. You have become so weak over the span of generations able to be counted on one hand, that returning to the animal kingdom, the world of weak and strong, survivor and prey, would easily prove to be your end.

We are the oppressors by inheritance, begging with our jowled throats thrust forward to be made into the victims.

THIS SHIP IS SINKING

This ship is sinking. Because it is hideously overcrowded and full of good intentions. We are getting tired and lazy and far too esoteric for our own survival; we are unable protect our own hides. We are like the eternal wife, trailer or welfare flat bound, whose shrill, wailing excuses for her drunken, oblivious common-law husband's ignorant, weak attacks are matched in impact only by the purple bruises ripening on her face and throat, or ever so slowly fading on her ageing mottled thighs. Who deserves the greater measure of disgust: the flatulent, impotent, bone-deep ignorant and piss-drunk wife-beater, the woman who chooses to carry, apologise for and eternally forgive this weak fuck that surely as salt on a plant will drain and kill her through stupid perseverance, or the cop who has to face their mutually assured destruction night after endless infecting night? How long can it go on?

You can pretend to care about your friend's problems if her boyfriend gets a little too nasty or a little too free with his hands. Its easy to schedule time as the appointed shoulder to cry on, as long as there is nothing more pressing than the apathetic routine filling up your most important cognitive hours with grey distraction. What do you know about being thrown into contact with examples of human behaviour so extreme, so disgusting and so awful that strangers have to call in appointed peace-keepers to whip the animals? Do you understand what it means to be the hand behind that whip? Can you imagine being the target of their unfocused rage and unpredictable, randomly expressed self-loathing?

The police are not conscripted; they choose their role.

Why would one choose this role, as a public servant earning a low-to-average wage, with no reward save the mute complacency of those they protect?

There are far easier ways to establish oneself as a sadist, as a bully or as a pseudo-saviour. To take on a task so thankless suggests an initial state of mind just as comfortable, candy-coated and muddled as the fog most of us exist through until the reaper tallies years lived against fatty, sugary crap ingested and whisks you off to see all of your dead buddies and childhood pets. A desire to do good, to protect and serve.

Only after prolonged and constant exposure to the worst, most selfish, ignorant, ugly, petty and evil faces of man might the germ of corruption take root. Whispering its gentle, logical, excusable case.

You see atrocities, you see lies and you see ignorant, mean behaviour every single night and every single day. Week in and week out of battered bloody victims, bodies destroyed by violence and abuse, auto-wrecks, abandoned babies, overdoses, suicides, murders. You develop instincts. Month in and month out of stinking homeless alcoholics, junkies, wife-beaters, thieves, rapists and killers. Year in and year out of confused victims, scared victims, shocked victims. Your moral barometer shifts, while you remain centred, if you are smart. If you are lucky. You can only help so much. Your family, the people that are actually real to you on a primal, neural level, have to take precedence over these weaklings that are so wilfully devolved that you have to decipher and solve their problems for them.

Imagine being judged by the pale, bug-eyed faces pulling aside the curtain of their fragile homes and pretending that they understand what they see.

Imagine that you were strong enough to stand up.

AUTHOR BIOGRAPHIES

JACK SARGEANT
Born in 1968, Jack Sargeant is author of numerous books on avant-garde and underground culture, including *Deathtripping: The Cinema Of Transgression*, *Naked Lens: Beat Cinema* (both Creation Books), and *Cinema Contra Cinema* (Fringecore). He is editor of the journal *Suture* and contributes to numerous publications, including *Headpress*, *Black Ice* and *Sleazenation*. Sargeant has recently devoted his time to editing two volumes of 'cratological mania': *Death Cults* (Virgin Books) and *Guns, Death, Terror* (Creation). He has toured widely, and his underground-and-outlaw-culture lectures and film-shows mix a twisted academic perception with occasional outbursts of virulent nihilism. He is fascinated by extremes of human behaviour.

CHRIS BARBER
Ex-Rent-Boy and Freelance Situationist, also part-time legal/trial adviser to criminals on remand.

MARTIN JONES
Martin Jones was born in Torquay in 1970. He has contributed to *Amygdala*; *Bedlam*; *Chaotic Order*; *Creeping Flesh*; *Headpress*; *My Bloody Valentine* (Virgin Books), *Necronomicon*; *Paperback Dungeon*; *Penthouse*; *Samhain*; *Shocking Cinema of the Seventies* (Noir Publishing) and *Usher*. He is the author of *Psychedelic Decadence: Sex, Drugs, Low-Art in 60s and 70s Britain* (Critical Vision), and the editor of *Lovers, Buggers and Thieves: Garage Rock, Monster Rock, Psychedelic Rock, Progressive Rock —* forthcoming from the same publishers. With the artist

Oliver Tomlinson he runs Omnium Gatherum Press, publishers of *Careful*, a comic so sinister that one would normally shun it (www.omniumgatherumpress.com).

RUSSELL GOULD
Russell Gould is a freelance writer and the author of *Unsolved Murders* (Virgin Books, 2000). He lives in London.

JOHN HARRISON
Weened from an early age on a steady diet of Marvel Comics, *Famous Monsters of Filmland* magazine, classic Hammer Horror and endless re-runs of *Hawaii Five-O*, Melbourne-based John Harrison has been working as a freelance writer for the past ten years, contributing pieces to such varied publications as *The Big Issue*; *Is it Uncut?* *Headpress*; *The Eros Journal*; *Metro*; *European Trash Cinema*; *Fatal Visions* and many others. He is also a regular writer for the Something Weird video company in Seattle, contributing video reviews for their website and catalogues. Harrison self-publishes *Hip Pocket Sleaze* – the guide to vintage adult paperbacks – a book-length version of which is due for publication by Headpress. Among his future projects is a reference work to Charles Manson-related material. He also runs The Graveyard Tramp, a small mail-order company specialising in horror and sleaze movie memorabilia, lurid paperbacks and pulps, true crime items, underground comics and other esoteric pieces of pop culture artefacts.

MIKITA BROTTMAN
Mikita Brottman is a professor of literature at the Maryland Institute College of Art. She is the author of *Offensive Films* (Greenwood, 1997), *Meat is Murder* (Creation, 1998, 2002). *Hollywood Hex* (Creation, 1999)

and the editor of *Car Crash Culture* (Palgrave, 2002). She writes frequently on film, crime and popular culture for both mainstream and alternative publications.

SIMON WHITECHAPEL

Simone Whitechapel was born in Madagascar, where he had an agnostic upbringing and trained as a librarian. Since his contributions to early editions of *Headpress* journal, his work has appeared in publications ranging from *Popular Astronomy* to *Chronicles of the Cthulhu Codex*. His books include *Crossing to Kill*, a study of serial killing in the Mexican border-city of Ciudad Juárez, re-issued in a revised edition by Virgin Books in 2002. His latest works, *Flesh Inferno: Atrocities of Torquemada and the Spanish Inquisition* and *Kamp Kulture: A History of Nazi Exploitation*, will be published by Creation Books in 2003. His interests include magic squares and closed-circuit television.

LANCE SINCLAIR

A thirty-year-old former music journalist operating from Queensland, Australia. His twin lifelong passions of film and true crime ephemera have given him a unique insight into the milieu of the contemporary lazy voyeur. He has contributed to *Death Cults* and the forthcoming *Guns, Death, Terror*.

**Look out for other compelling,
all-new True Crime titles from Virgin Books**

MY BLOODY VALENTINE
Couples Whose Sick Crimes Shocked the World
Edited by Patrick Blackden

Good-looking Canadian couple Paul Bernardo and Karla
Homolka looked the epitome of young, wholesome success.
No one could have guessed that they drugged, raped and
murdered young women to satisfy Bernardo's deviant lusts.
Nothing inspires more horror and fascination than couples
possessed of a single impulse – to kill for thrills. Obsessed by
and sucked into their own sick and private madness, their
attraction is always fatal, their actions always desperate. The
book covers a variety of notorious killer couples: from
desperados Starkweather and Fugate, on whom the film
Natural Born Killers was based, right through to Fred and Rose
West, who committed unspeakable horrors in their semi-
detached house in Gloucester, England. With contributions
from a variety of leading true crime journalists, *My Bloody
Valentine* covers both the world-famous cases and also lesser
known but equally horrifying crimes.

£7.99 ISBN: 0-7535-0647-5

DEATH CULTS
Murder, Mayhem and Mind Control
Edited by Jack Sargeant

Throughout history thousands of people have joined cults and even committed acts of atrocity in the belief they would attain power and everlasting life. From Charles Manson's 'family' of the late 1960s to the horrific Ten Commandments of God killings in Uganda in March 2000, deluded and brainwashed followers of cults and their charismatic megalomaniac leaders have been responsible for history's most shocking and bizarre killings. Jack Sargeant has compiled twelve essays featuring cults about whom very little has previously been written, such as the Russian castration sect and the bizarre Japanese Aum doomsday cult that leaked sarin gas into Tokyo's subways.

£7.99 ISBN: 0-7535-0644-0

DANGER DOWN UNDER
The Dark Side of the Australian Dream
Patrick Blackden

Australia is one of the most popular long-haul tourist destinations, but its image of a carefree, 'no worries' culture set in a landscape of stunning natural beauty tells only one side of the story. *Danger Down Under* lets you know what the tourist board won't – the dark side of the Australian dream. With a landscape that can be extremely hostile to those unfamiliar to its size and extremes, and an undying macho culture – not to mention the occasional psychotic who murders backpackers, or crazed gangs of bikers and cultists – there is much to be cautious of when venturing down under.

£7.99 ISBN 0-7535-0649-1

DIRTY CASH
Organised Crime in the Twenty First Century
David Southwell

There was once only one Mafia: now every country seems to have its own. Until fairly recently gangsters kept to their territories, but crime – like every other business – has been quick to take advantage of the new global economy. Business, it seems, is good, with over $150 billion laundered each year in Europe alone. As links are formed between the Mafia, the Triads, the Yardies, the Yakuza, the Russian Mafiya and the South American cartels, a tide of misery spreads throughout the world. The book looks in detail at the specific groups involved, the horrifying crimes they commit, and the everyday lives of their members.

£7.99 ISBN: 07535 0702 1

TEENAGE RAMPAGE
The Worldwide Youth Crime Explosion
Antonio Mendoza

Columbine High School, Colorado, Spring 1999. Twelve of its schoolchildren and one teacher lay dead. Two boys have gone on a killing spree, venting their anger at their classmates before turning their guns on themselves. Cases such as Columbine are occurring with increasing regularity – and guns are not always involved. In Japan in 1998, a 13-year old schoolboy murdered his teacher in a frenzied knife attack. What is happening in society that young people are running amok, fuelled by hatred and nihilism, with little regard for their own lives and the lives of those around them? Expert crime writer Antonio Mendoza investigates this worldwide problem and comes up with some shocking findings that call for a global rethink on how we bring up – and punish – those responsible for the worldwide teenage crimewave.

£7.99 ISBN: 07535 0715 3

FEMALE TERROR
Scary Women, Modern Crimes
Ann Magma

Statistics show that female crime and female violence is on the rise, particularly in America where, in 1999, over two million violent female offenders were recorded and the rise was cited as 137 per cent. Women are becoming an ever-growing presence in crime statistics, becoming a major force in both organised crime and terrorism. In the last ten years they have also come to the fore as homicidal leaders of religious sects and gun-toting leaders of Los Angeles street gangs, whose members are every bit as tough and violent as their male 'gangsta' counterparts. From Ulrike Meinhof to Wafa Idris; from IRA terrorists to Mafia godmothers, this book will look at the rise and rise of female terror.

£7.99 ISBN: 07535 0718 8

MONSTERS OF DEATH ROW
America's Dead Men and Women Walking
Christopher Berry-Dee and Tony Brown

From the cells of Death Row come the chilling, true-life accounts of the most heinous, cruel and depraved killers of modern times. At the time of writing, there are 3,702 inmates on Death Row across the USA, many of who have caused their victims to consciously suffer agonising physical pain and tortuous mental anguish before death. These are not normal human beings. They have carried out serial murder, mass-murder, spree killing, necrophdia, and dismemberment of bodies – both dead and alive. In these pages are to be found fiends who have stabbed, hacked, set fire to, and even filleted their victims. So meet the 'dead men and women walking' in the most terrifying true crime read ever.

£7.99 ISBN 07535 0722 6

WHEN KIDS KILL

Jonathan Paul

Cases of child homicide are rare but, as we all know, they are especially horrific and tap directly into adult fears about the end of innocence and the potential harm of violent TV programmes and computer games. In this topical yet sensitive investigation Jonathan Paul goes behind the sensational headlines that dominated crimes such as the Bulger killing to argue that children are not 'born killers', but that evil is learned, not innate. The author asks why such unthinkable crimes happen and examines child homicide both in today's violent, confusing world and against the cruel, unforgiving retribution of yesterday. This is what happens when childhood is trodden underfoot: this is when – and why – kids kill.

£7.99 ISBN 07535 0758 7

The best in true crime from Virgin Books

How to order by mail:
Tick the box for the title/s you wish to order and complete the form overleaf. Please do not forget to include your address.

Please send me the books I have ticked above.

Please enclose a cheque or postal order, made payable to Virgin Books Ltd, to the value of the books you have ordered plus postage and packing costs as follows:

UK and BFPO – £1.00 for the first book, 50p for each subsequent book.

Overseas (including Republic of Ireland) – £2.00 for the first book, £1.00 for each subsequent book.

If you would prefer to pay by VISA, ACCESS/MASTERCARD, DINERS CLUB, AMEX or SWITCH, please write your card number and expiry date here

Card no.

Expiry date:

Signature

Send to: Cash Sales, Virgin Books, Thames Wharf Studios. Rainville Road, London, W6 9HA Please allow 28 days for delivery.

Name

Address

Post Code